CONTEMPORARY ISSUES IN
SOCIAL WORK: WESTERN EUROPE

BY THE SAME AUTHORS

Doel, M. and Shardlow, S.M. (1993) *Social Work Practice*, Aldershot: Gower.

Doel, M. and Shardlow, S.M. (eds) (1996) *Social Work in a Changing World: An International Perspective on Practice Learning*, Aldershot: Arena.

Doel, M. and Shardlow, S.M. (1998) *The New Social Work Practice* , Aldershot: Arena.

Doel, M., Shardlow, S.M., Sawdon, C. and Sawdon, D. (1996) *Teaching Social Work Practice*, Aldershot: Arena.

Payne, M. (1979) *Power, Authority and Responsibility in Social Services: Social Work in Area Teams*, Basingstoke: Macmillan.

Payne, M. (1982) *Working in Teams*, Basingstoke: Macmillan.

Payne, M. (1986) *Social Care in the Community*, Basingstoke: Macmillan.

Payne, M. (1991) *Modern Social Work Theory: A Critical Introduction*, Basingstoke: Macmillan.

Payne, M. (1993) *Linkages: Effective Networking in Social Care*, London: Whiting and Birch.

Payne, M. (1995) *Social Work and Community Care*, Basingstoke: Macmillan.

Payne, M. (1996) *What is Professional Social Work?*, Birmingham: Venture.

Payne, M. and Arkley, S. (eds) (1991) *SEARCH: The Social Services Consultancy and Training Directory, 1991–2*, Birmingham: BASW Trading.

Payne, M. and Arkley, S. (eds) (1993) *SEARCH: The Social Services and Community Care Consultancy and Training Directory, 1993–4*, Birmingham: BASW Trading.

Shardlow, S.M. (ed.) (1989) *The Values of Change in Social Work*, London: Routledge.

Shardlow, S.M. and Doel, M. (1996) *Practice Learning and Teaching*, Basingstoke: Macmillan.

Contemporary Issues in Social Work

Western Europe

Edited by Steven Shardlow and Malcolm Payne

Published by
Arena
Ashgate Publishing Limited
Gower House
Croft Road
Aldershot
Hants GU11 3HR
England

Ashgate Publishing Company
Old Post Road
Brookfield
Vermont 05036
USA

British Library Cataloguing in Publication Data
Contemporary issues in social work: Western Europe
    1. Social service – Europe
    I. Shardlow, Steven, 1952–   II. Payne, Malcolm
    361.3'094

    ISBN 1 85742 427 1

Library of Congress Cataloging-in-Publication Data
Contemporary issues in social work: Western Europe/edited by Steven
  Shardlow and Malcolm Payne.
     p. cm.
  Includes bibliographical references and index.
  ISBN 1-85742-427-1
  1. Social services—Europe, Western.   I. Shardlow, Steven, 1952–
  II. Payne, Malcolm, 1947– .
HV240.5.C65   1997
361.3'2'094—dc21
                                                          97–19653
                                                           CIP

Typeset in Palatino by Raven Typesetters, Chester
Printed and bound in Great Britain by MPG Books Ltd, Bodmin, Cornwall

For social work practitioners across Europe.

Contents

List of tables

Acknowledgements

A very large number of people have been involved in writing and producing this book. It is impossible to acknowledge their contributions individually: indeed, the names of many of those who have contributed to the development of this book are unknown to us. Therefore we would like to thank all who have worked together on this project: writers, translators, secretaries, and those who have provided support and inspiration. There is one person we must single out for special mention and gratitude: Marg Walker, our secretary, based in Sheffield.

We would also like to gratefully acknowledge the financial support of the Association of Teachers in Social Work Education, Joint Universities Council Social Work Education Committee and Manchester Metropolitan University. Without their support this venture would not have been possible.

Notes on contributors

Anna Maria Cavallone is a social work consultant. After several years in social work teaching, she works in a central government agency responsible for a programme of technical assistance and accreditation of social work schools. She also engaged in studies on social work functions and tasks, and in reports and action for the development of social work education. For several years she served on the board of IASSW and of ICSW, and is still engaged in the activities of ICSW.

Tine Egelund is a social worker. She is head of the continuing education programme at the School of Social Work in Copenhagen, where she is study adviser for the masters programme. She has been a lecturer at all levels of social education, has worked as a supervisor and consultant in social institutions, and has undertaken research on the social work of municipal administrations. She has published a number of articles and textbooks concerning social work, and is currently working on a thesis at the University of Lund.

Josefina Fernández is a social worker and lawyer, and is a professor at the University of Barcelona's School of Social Work, as well as acting as a supervisor in a mental health centre. Her professional activities have included different social work positions in the mental health field and in children's departments. She has also held various teaching positions and given technical support to the voluntary sector. She has produced a number of publications related to social work.

Franca Ferrario is an expert in social work methodology. She is engaged in teaching at the School of Social Work at Turin University and in permanent education programmes. She is also active as a social work consultant, and is the author of several books (*Territorio e servizio sociale*, Unicopli, Milan, 1987;

Il lavoro di gruppo con gli adolescenti, NIS, Rome, 1990; *Il lavoro di rete nel servizio sociale*, NIS, Rome, 1992).

Therese Halskov is a social worker. For many years, she was head of basic education at the School of Social Work in Copenhagen. Today she is a lecturer and researcher in social work. Her research themes have mainly been quality development in social work in the municipal administrations, and social work with single mothers in a European comparative perspective. She has published a number of articles and textbooks about social work.

David Kramer is Professor of Social Policy and Vice-rector of the Alice-Salomon-Fachhochschule, Berlin. From 1986 to 1993 he was director for Europe of the German Marshall Fund of the United States. His primary academic interests are in the history of social work/social policy, international comparative social work/social policy, and the use of new technologies in social work and social work education. He has directed several programme evaluation exercises commissioned by governmental and private organizations. He was director of studies of the Council of Europe's 1994/95 co-ordinated research in the social field on the initial and further training of social workers, taking into account their changing role.

Geert van der Laan is a social psychologist at the Netherlands Institute of Care and Welfare, Utrecht. He is also Professor of Social Work at the University of Utrecht. His current research interests are in the following areas: accountability in social work, the quality of communication and information systems, case-based reasoning, the relationship between material and non-material problems, and the democratic use of professional power.

Ann Lavan is a lecturer in social policy and social work at University College, Dublin. Her experience includes social work practice in mental health and community work in the United Kingdom and Ireland. She was a member of the Commission on Social Welfare and served on the board of the Combat Poverty Agency (in Ireland). She was a founder member of the European Association of Schools of Social Work and has been a member of the board of the International Association of Schools of Social Work. She is Book Review Editor of *International Social Work*.

Alcina Monteiro is a social worker. She has worked for several years in the area of community work and in a general hospital. Since 1978, she has also taught at the Higher Institute of Social Work in Oporto in the areas of placements, social administration and theory, and the methodology of social work. She has been a member of the institute's managing board for the past ten years. Her research interests are social policy and new agents for welfare provision. She is currently enrolled in the PhD programme of the Catholic University of São Paulo, Brazil.

Malcolm Payne is Professor and Head of Applied Community Studies at the Manchester Metropolitan University. He previously worked in probation, the social services and in the local and national voluntary sector in the UK. He is the author of *Modern Social Work Theory* (Macmillan, Basingstoke, 1991, 1997), *Social Work and Community Care* (Macmillan, Basingstoke, 1995) and *What is Professional Social Work?* (Venture, Birmingham, 1996).

Robert Ploem studied economics and social psychology, and has carried out advanced studies in tutoring and supervision. He is a senior lecturer and tutor at the School of Social Work of the Hogeschool van Amsterdam, and he is also an independent consultant and writer. He is a member of the board of editors of *Supervisie in Opleiding en Beroep*, a quarterly on tutoring and supervision. He is also a member of the advisory board of *Social Work in Europe*.

Tim Robinson is a lecturer in social work at the University of Sheffield, with particular responsibility for community care teaching. He has experience in hospital social work and with a family-based respite care project. He is a consumer of community care services as the carer for a daughter with spina bifida. He is Vice-chair of the Services Committee of the Association for Spina Bifida and Hydrocephalus.

Fernanda Rodrigues is a social worker and a sociologist. She has worked in social security in the field of supplementary benefits, and as evaluator of the Portuguese projects linked with the European Union Anti-Poverty Programme (Poverty III). She is also a teacher at the Higher Institute of Social Work in Oporto, in the areas of placements, social policy and theory, and the methodology of social work. She has been a member of its managing board for the past eight years, and is co-ordinator of post-qualification courses. At present, she is Municipal Director for Housing and Social Development for the city of Oporto. Her current research interests are in the following areas: social policy, public assistance, poverty and local action and social development. She is working on her PhD thesis at the University of São Paulo, Brazil.

Teresa Rossell is a social worker and psychologist. She is the director and professor of the University of Barcelona's School of Social Work. She is the author of *The Interview in Social Work* and has published contributions to journals and conferences on social work and social work education. She has participated in research on subjects related to volunteer motivations and social work tasks, among others. She has been a member of the Executive Committee of the IASSW, and from 1991 to 1995 she was President of the

European Association of Schools of Social Work. She has also been nomi-
nated as Honorary Professor of the St Petersburg University of Humanities
and Social Sciences. She has been participating in and promoting the European dimension of social policy through the ERASMUS, TEMPUS and
TACIS programmes.

Steven Shardlow is Director of the MA/Diploma in Applied Social Studies
at the University of Sheffield, where he is also Director of the Diploma in
Practice Teaching. He is the former Chairperson of the Association of Teachers in Social Work Education. He is joint editor of the journal *Issues in Social
Work Education*. He is a member of the Executive Committee of the European
Association of Schools of Social Work. His current research interests are in
the following areas: comparative social work practice; social work education,
especially practice learning, and social work values and ethics. He has
published widely in these fields, and his work has been translated into
several languages.

June Thoburn is Professor of Social Work and Director of the School of Social
Work and the Centre for Research on the Child and Family at the University
of East Anglia, Norwich. She has worked as a social worker in Canada and
England. Her teaching interests include child and family social work policy,
planning and practice, and international aspects of child welfare provision.
Her book *Child Placement: Principles and Practice* (Arena, Aldershot, 1994)
emphasizes the importance of empowerment strategies and participatory
methods. She has written widely about her research on child protection and
child placement.

Jo Thompson is Co-chair of the National Association of Probation Officers, a
professional association and trade union representing over 7,500 staff in
England, Wales and Northern Ireland. She trained as a probation officer in
1974, and works as a senior probation officer in Nottinghamshire Probation
Service. As a main-grade and senior probation officer, she has worked in
field teams, a 'rehabilitation' team, the crown court, magistrates' court and in
group work.

1 Exploring social work in Europe

Malcolm Payne and Steven Shardlow

Two questions: How? and Why?

In this book, we aim to explore social work in Europe. This has raised two questions for us, which we want to consider in this chapter. How can we understand social work in Europe? Why should we do so? The answers to these questions have influenced how we have organized the book and its contributions. Both questions also raise complex issues about understanding in general and comparative study in particular, and we consider some of these in the next few paragraphs.

Britain is our home country, and the place where we undertook our professional training and practice. We have lived there between us for the best part of a hundred years, and been involved in social work for fifty of them. Our understanding of social work in Britain is, as a result, of a special quality. We have met and communicated with British people every day of our lives, we speak the language, we have learned to live within its social conventions, we have experienced daily its social and political life, and we have accumulated memories of the period we have lived through. Our understanding of social work is placed within the context of our language, human experience, professional training and personal and academic preference and prejudice. Our knowledge of other countries' social work can never achieve such depth and sophistication by being incorporated in our social experience in this way. This will also be true for many readers who 'know' their own social work system and its context.

We therefore 'know' British social work and its political and social context in a way that we can 'know' no other. In dealing with comparative accounts of social work in other countries, this represents a problem. Many equally 'knowing' people would dispute our knowledge because they 'know' it differently. In spite of the depth of our knowledge and understanding, we can never know it completely or from every angle. Particular faults in the

1

geology of our understanding might arise because we experience our social world and social work as white males. Different ethnic groups and women might experience Britain's social world and its social work completely differently because of the particular social pressures on their worlds. Many other social and personal differences might have an influence. These different forms of social experience are expressed in academic, ideological and professional debates about the nature of social work in Britain.

Much of our knowing does not come from a firm certainty about what British social work 'is' or 'is like', but from an awareness of the various debates which are in progress. One of us has argued elsewhere (Payne, 1996) that social work is a discourse among different points of view, and may be understood and 'known' as such, rather than being a social reality which we may understand completely.

We have argued, then, that no individual can 'know' a complex aspect of social life such as social work adequately. So how can we hope to 'know' about social work in another country where we do not even have the social experience and depth of professional learning that we have about our own country? If social work is its discourse, we cannot know about a discourse in languages and social experiences other than our own, so this seems to make comparative study even more hopeless. However, Brown (1994), in her account of teaching comparative social work in a British social work course, argues that seeing alternative perspectives tends to lead us to act sceptically, defensively or with amazement. She suggests that if we are not simply to marvel or reject, we need to have a very clear framework of analysis of differences that we can perceive, and we need to explore carefully how real these differences are. In comparing different services, she proposes a focus on the welfare ideology which lies behind it, the country's economic position, relevant demographic factors, religious and ideological demands, and the nature of social work. Many of these factors emerge in the accounts in this book as central to understanding a particular nation's social work.

This view, then, proposes that it is not hopeless to study social work comparatively, but we must not simply accept surface accounts of sameness and difference, but try to understand with precision the origins and structures of particular aspects of social work within the social context of the relevant countries. Helping such a process is one of the aims of this book. We do not seek to cover everything to do with social welfare, and we have not sought to impose a 'British' perspective on what to compare. Instead, we have started from the current issues and contemporary debates in specified countries in a small area of the social services – the personal social services. We have sought what is, in effect, a 'position statement' from well-known social work educators or professionals in each country, and the account follows their priorities and concerns, the issues that they see expressed in their country. While we have set up a similar format for each chapter, we have not sought to constrain the balance of emphasis and priority given in the account which emerges from each country. Thus, the reader is not presented with a set of easily comparable categories of information on which to make simplistic judgements. They have, instead, a contextualized account of what seems important to a protagonist in that country's discourse. Starting from this, they may make their own explorations by analysis of specific areas of interest to them.

This leads us to the question 'Why?' If comparative study is so difficult and likely to be barren of achievement, why bother to explore European social work? One reason, expressed by Lorenz (1994), is that we have moved beyond the nation state, and that Europe should now be our horizon. For him, social workers will naturally want to know about social work beyond their immediate needs. Our context is no longer just our own nation state, but the political and social context: Europe. Perhaps, as globalization advances, it will become the world. To understand what we are doing more completely, we must try to understand this aspect of our environment. The problem with this view, however, is that it is perfectly possible to operate for most of the time without paying attention to fairly distant activities in different countries. Social work can be practised in a particularly culture-bound way, because of the strong influence of national policy and legal imperatives.

Some arguments about the desirability and necessity of studying social work and social services in Europe hinge on the social changes that membership of the European Union will, and is intended to, bring about in this culture-bound view. Membership is intended to increase the mobility of the workforce, and this will lead to more clients of social services coming from across Europe. They will also move to other parts of Europe, so that Northumbrian social workers will have to have contact with colleagues from the foreign parts of Niarchos as well as Northampton when children on the child abuse register move on. Border controls are reducing, and this means that it will be easier for offenders to go missing in other countries, for parents without the care of their children to kidnap them and cross to other countries, and for runaways from home to move to Munich or Salerno rather than Manchester or Southend (not that they usually do any of these; they usually stay near home). Whereas unemployed young people have often tended to end up in Blackpool or Torquay for the summer, hoping perhaps to find casual work, they might think that it is warmer, drier and more exotic to sleep on the beach at Barcelona or Torremolinos (and that there's more work). Middle-class children have always done this, and there seems no reason why others should not.

But at least at present, the problems that this might cause are a bit distant, so the 'need to know' argument is not too strong. Clients have not really shown much tendency to move around Britain, let alone across Europe. Britain is still an island, language teaching is poor to non-existent, and it is comparatively expensive to get anywhere else in Europe because you have to pay the cost of crossing to mainland Europe. No social security system is all that helpful to people from other countries, and many people find that the police in most countries, as in Britain, are not too sympathetic and kindly to 'layabout foreigners' who are not spending money. The telephone system is quite good, the fax is ubiquitous, and fortunately, other European social workers are quite likely to speak English or to be able to find someone who can, so communication should not be too much of a problem.

If social workers do not 'need to know' about Europe in order to practise, the argument for understanding European social work as a social context loses some importance. But not wholly. The operation of the EU, with its increasingly common social and economic policies, will mean increasing commonality of social provision and priority (despite Britain's opt-out from the Social Chapter of the Maastricht Treaty, Denmark's other opt-outs, and the process of assimilation for newly-joining countries which means that participation is variable). Other countries are likely to join these structures. This political entity, which may soon develop shared foreign and defence policies, is one of the most coherent and strongly integrated of the regional groupings of countries. Similar but less formally-established entities are appearing throughout the world, on the Pacific rim, in Australasia, among Islamic countries in the Middle East, in Latin America, in sub-Saharan Africa, in Southern Africa and between Canada, Mexico and the USA. For readers outside the European Union, therefore, this account of the consequences for social work of developing 'regional' – that is, sub-continental – political and economic entities may come to prove a crucial case study presaging events world-wide. And in Eastern Europe, a newly-developing social work profession can look more closely at their colleagues' roles within the political and economic union they may soon join. Nordic countries, whose welfare states have been particularly comprehensive, may also observe the development of this important political entity, whether they are in it (as Finland and Sweden are) or whether they reject its clutches (as Norway recently has).

A further value of comparative study for us all is to help us ask questions. The importance of legal, political and historical context makes wholesale adoption of a model of practice from another country unlikely. However, what is done elsewhere can raise questions about our nation's approach to particular issues and its value, provided, as we have argued, we do not simply marvel or reject, but examine and analyse rigorously. Armstrong and Hollows's (1991) paper on responses to child abuse is an example of such analysis. They show that some similar issues arise throughout Europe, but that responses to them vary. Britain's largely legalistic and bureaucratic system can be contrasted with Holland's more therapeutic and confidential system. This gives the lie to those who would claim in any country that 'there is no alternative'. Somewhere, we may always find an operating alternative, and it may illuminate our blind spots and prejudices. Armstrong and

Hollows create a model of the interaction of denial of the problem, social attitudes to children and families, and the definition of abuse, to explain variations in practice and definition.

Yet Armstrong and Hollows's paper also exemplifies a problem in making comparisons between countries: the centrality of denial, attitudes and definition draws attention to it, and their conclusion hints at it. They say that for the benefit of children we must develop a shared approach, particularly when we will be dealing with more mobile populations, and give attention to the welfare of children as individuals, and the role of families in rearing them. A European response must be developed. Hidden here is a view that one cultural approach should be triumphant, that putting children at the centre of our response will inevitably be seen as right, whatever our cultural and national tradition. Comments on Italy's 'reluctance' to develop therapeutic programmes, criticisms of the Irish rejection of the concept of abuse (which they acknowledge is a social construction to identify and understand aspects of behaviour towards children) and their emphasis on the need to 'accept' the concept of abuse show how difficult it is to divorce oneself from the assumption that one's own perspective is correct, while at the same time seeking to understand something of others' views.

The chapters in this book do not seek to make comparisons of this kind, which require detailed analyses of particular aspects of social services provision and practice. They are concerned, instead, to provide an overall context for such comparative evaluations, and to provide a starting point for further exploration in the social work literature and discourse in other countries. We also seek to stimulate readers to ask themselves questions about their own practice and policy by seeing that practice and policy in another context may, entirely reasonably, be different or even opposed to their own.

The approach of this volume, then, is to provide a particular comparative resource. It should enable the study of social work as a whole, and its progress (or lack of it), in various Western European countries. This offers a context for later more detailed exploration in European social work in specific areas, reacting to specific questions which readers may want to ask themselves. We hope it will prove useful in this way, and stimulating in allowing countries to ask themselves about their own social work. We specifically reject the possibility of 'knowing' social work in other countries, as we can 'know' our own in a contextualized way, and we point to the reality that we cannot 'know' our own social work from every point of view, but only specific parts of it, and the discourses about it and those parts. Thus, the lack of 'knowing' about social work in other countries is no more than a reflection, enlarged, of our inability to 'know' our own social work from every point of view.

Britain in Europe

The British reader may be surprised to find a chapter on Britain in this book. What is the point of an account of British social work when we want to explore Europe? It is here for three reasons. First, this book will be sold throughout the world, and readers in the English-speaking world are likely to find Britain just as worthy of exploration as any other European country. Related to that reason, they may find access to the British texts and the British context easier, being English-speaking, and perhaps become more familiar with the British literature and context through the opportunity to read it. So gaining access to European social work may be made easier by having access to a chapter on British social work. We invite British readers to look on the contribution about Britain as a challenge to their insularity and international-ism, by looking at Britain anew to see what its recent social work history might offer to other countries, and to gain a wider perspective on its weak-nesses.

Second, we seek to draw attention to the constraints of the other chapters by giving British readers a taste of the medicine which we have forced on the contributors from mainland Europe: British readers may find a brief account of an interpretation of the main trends in British social work over the past few years. To the extent that they can 'know' about British social work, they can judge the extent to which the constraints of a chapter in this book prevent or enable an adequate picture of a country's provision. They can therefore 'know' something more about the other countries represented here by being better able to judge how their own country fares within these constraints.

Third, and most important, we are making a controversial and political point. Britain is, we say, part of Europe. It is part of a set of traditions and history, a culture which is recognizably that of Western Europe. It is socially part of Europe. We originally chose the countries represented in this book from a political entity: the European Union. The involvement of countries in the union, the way it should develop, the role it plays in political and daily life and the nature and role of its institutions are controversial in many of them, perhaps particularly so in Britain. Thus, Britain is not only socially but politically involved in, and therefore part of, Europe, if not the EU. Therefore, choosing a set of countries from this political entity is a statement about Britain's part in it. We have discussed above the importance of the develop-ment of regional, sub-continental economic and political entities. Our focus on Europe accepts that, whether this is resisted in Britain or elsewhere, this is a characteristic of economic and political globalization in the late twentieth century.

The organization of the book

This book is the first of a series that we intend to edit. Therefore, it does not seek to cover the whole of Europe, but only to represent a part of the European experience of social work.

We selected a number of countries within the European Union at the time we started the book. Several countries have joined since. A selection was necessary, because covering each of the then nine, now fifteen, soon probably more, countries would have made the book unwieldy and expensive.

We have tried to offer accounts of countries' social work services that allow some comparisons of countries with similar stages of development, some related histories, and some contrasts between countries with rather different histories. Ireland and the UK, for example, are neighbours on a group of islands, and share some aspects of history, and English as a language in common use, as important links, but there are also significant differences, in size, development and in the role of the Catholic Church. Denmark, Germany and the Netherlands are other Northern European countries with some shared boundaries, histories and common traditions, but many historic conflicts and differences. Portugal and Spain share the same peninsula, some linguistic commonality, a recent history of dictatorship and political reform, relatively belated development of the social services and, again, a significant role for the Catholic Church. Italy, another Southern European country, has many similar features, although its social services have a longer post-1945 history in the mainstream of international development.

We hope, therefore, that the reader will see resonances, similarities, oppositions and differences.

We approached authors in each of the countries selected, gave them a similar brief and have edited their contributions into a similar form. Thus, we hope to offer a series of contributions that allow some comparisons and links to be drawn, but we have not expected the writers to do this. For example, some writers concentrate more on direct practice, others on education. Our final chapter tries to draw out of the contributions some continuities and differences among the countries. The brief asked authors to identify major trends in social work services in their country within recent years, placing these in historical context. We asked them to refer to major pieces of research, major legislative and service organization developments, and to indicate some resources of literature which would allow a reader to make a start in exploring their countries' social work services further. We also asked them to discuss how social work education prepared students for social work practice.

The balance between the elements of social work practice, social service legislation and organization, and social work education varies according to the emphasis and importance given to them by the authors. The authors also chose how to represent their own countries' developments. Sometimes, they have done so by dealing with some aspects of service or specializations as examples of wider developments. Sometimes, they have offered less detailed accounts of a wider range of issues. Of course, the authors' approach and position in their countries' academic debate is their own, although they were asked to represent the range of views fairly. However, in their argument you can often see their own personal or regional experience and interests and their own academic views and arguments coming through. We have valued this small indication for the reader from elsewhere of the sense of debate and controversy within each country. It allows the expression of some of the 'discourse' which constructs social work in each country.

Each chapter is then organized in a common sequence, although each has its own balance and headings. There is, first, an introduction which offers an overview of the organization and main themes of the chapter. This is followed by a brief historical context. Then there is a discussion of some important areas of social work practice, involving explanation about administrative organization and legal constraints, although as far as possible this is separated out and follows the account of practice issues. A section on social work education follows, and then there is a drawing together of themes and issues identified as important by the authors. A bibliography and also a wider account of sources in each country can be found at the end of the book, organized by chapter.

After this introductory chapter, the eight countries are presented in alphabetical order of the Anglicized country name. The book is completed in Chapter 10 by our analysis of issues and themes which arise throughout the chapters, which is offered with the aim of making a start on identifying unifying and conflicting themes across social work in Europe.

In editing this book, we are aware of the many difficulties of establishing accurate communication across linguistic national and cultural boundaries. It is no mere matter of taking the words written in one language and simply translating them into another language. Many ideas and concepts are unique to the society in which they are found. We have sought through the translation and editing processes to allow the voices of the authors in the book to be heard in all of their timbre, tone and range of expression. Sometimes this may mean that the English is not entirely idiomatic. This represents an attempt to capture the essence of meaning expressed by the author.

There are particular problems in finding a correct term for some ideas: take, for example, the collective noun used to refer to people who may or may not currently live in houses but who have a history of travelling and share an ethnic identity. In some parts of Europe they might be referred to as Romanies or Gypsies: these terms might or might not be seen as pejorative, either by the groups referred to or by the wider population. In the United Kingdom

– and we take this country because it is most familiar to us – these terms would be seen as pejorative, and another term, Travellers, has become more widely accepted. We have followed the convention of using the term, in translation, that is used in the country being discussed – the voice of the author is given freedom of expression unless to do so would be misleading. We believe this to be a more accurate representation of reality than to impose the current usage of one country, the UK, on others within the EU, unless to do so would cause gross offence to the community of those who understand English and who may read this book.

Therefore, as editors, we have sought to adopt a position of balance. No doubt for some readers we will not always get the balance correct. Not that these are the only problems of translating meaning. For example, the term 'Traveller' has a broader meaning than 'Romany', as 'Traveller' is used to refer to all those who have a travelling lifestyle, and not only to people who share a similar ethnicity through language, culture and religion. Thus terms are often not coterminous – the Dutch *Hogescholen* are similar to but not the same as German *Fachhochschulen*, and neither has an equivalent in current English because these types of institutions do not exist in the United Kingdom. Where translation is impossible, we have continued to use the Dutch, German or whatever other language's word is necessary to refer to the entity in question. It behoves us all to exercise caution against a common tendency to seek similarity and familiarity where in reality there is only tentative resemblance.

2 Social work in Denmark

Therese Halskov and Tine Egelund

Translated by Karin Thrysøe

Introduction

In this chapter, we will first present a brief overview of those themes in social policy which have been dominant since 1990: experimental and development strategies, 'activation' initiatives, and the development of interest in the voluntary and private sectors. Then we will look at the situation in relation to children and special disadvantaged groups: ethnic minorities and mentally ill persons. In our account of the current situation in Denmark, we will also examine the work functions of social workers, changes in their education, and current debates in these areas. We will describe, in particular, discussions taking place concerning both basic professional education and the development of masters programmes.

Social policy change: The context

Denmark has a population of 5.2 million; about 2.9 million form the working population, some 45 per cent of whom are women. Since 1990, the unemployment rate has been rising, and is now in excess of 10 per cent of the working population. Like other Nordic countries, Denmark has provided generous levels of social welfare support for its population.

A major social policy reform project took place between 1988 and 1992. During this period the Folketing (the Danish parliament) appropriated 350 million Danish kroner for experimental, innovative projects in the field of social welfare. The Folketing defined the objectives of the programme as follows:

> to strengthen local initiatives and promote reform and preventive measures in the field of social welfare. The development programme seeks to promote locally-

based development work with a view both to strengthening the identity of local communities and to help break down barriers between generations. The programme aims at creating better opportunities for individual self-expression and participation in decision-making processes which affect people's daily lives. The programme will contribute to the prevention and resolution of social problems across sectional, administrative and occupational divisions.

Furthermore, a number of special priority themes were singled out as being of special interest to the politicians:

- children, young people and their families;
- groups with a need for activities and rehabilitation;
- elderly persons;
- groups with special needs (for instance, refugees/immigrants, disabled persons, excluded persons/homeless persons);
- local community and administrative projects.

These social development funds (SDFs, in Danish: SUM) were placed in a central pool under the Ministry for Social Affairs and, in principle, it was possible for all interested parties (public institutions, private organizations, voluntary bodies and individuals) to present ideas for projects and apply for funds from this pool to implement them. During the course of the programme, support was granted to 1,800 small and large pilot projects. It was a condition of receiving financial aid that all the projects supported were subsequently evaluated. In the years since 1991, a comprehensive comparative study has been undertaken to evaluate the experiences in connection with this reform. This evaluation study was published in 1992 (Flex and Nielsen, 1992; Jensen, 1992).

The official background leading to the introduction of a programme of this nature was that the key characteristics of the Scandinavian welfare model (a strong social state, the predominance of public social policy initiatives, with only little emphasis on the role of the market and the private sector in the social policy field, and central planning of the standards of social policy initiatives) had become too expensive – at least in the opinion of some of the leading political parties. Criticism was also voiced about the lack of substantive results from the welfare state: it was argued that the state did not stimulate, but rather discouraged, self-help processes in society. Therefore, the government sought to create an experimental culture, based on local needs in social work, with a higher degree of involvement at the local level to develop partnerships with private organizations, popular movements and voluntary organizations and individuals, and work across sectional lines with a view to establishing preventive measures with better possibilities for evaluation of needs, initiatives and costs in relation to each other.

This reform programme should be seen in the context of some important changes which have taken place in society. Throughout the 1980s, the level of unemployment became very high and a large minority of adults were socially excluded or marginalized. Also, demographic changes have resulted in an ageing population with special needs for support and care. Conditions for bringing up children for lone parents and parents at the lower end of the wage scale are difficult. Large middle-class groups – 'ordinary' unemployed persons, old people, families, etc. – have been proletarianized, turned into risk groups, excluded from daily social life, and are now in need of some form of support or assistance. The largest political problem in Denmark has been how to respond to the many ordinary people who have ended up in a more marginalized and unfavourable position in society. It is not possible to deal with these groups by means of the traditional approaches in social work. This would be far too expensive, and a democratic impossibility in relation to groups which do not see themselves as clients of social welfare. It is our opinion, although not necessarily in line with the official reasons stated, that these social developments have been the major driving force behind the development of a higher degree of welfare pluralism and new working methods in the field of social work. Yet the primary target groups of these reforms have perhaps not been the most disadvantaged groups in our society.

The subsequent very comprehensive evaluations of the reform programme have experienced considerable difficulties in measuring the results precisely. One clear conclusion that can be drawn is that it has been difficult for the projects initiated to reach out to most disadvantaged groups. This also applies to projects which specifically target those groups. These evaluations have also raised questions about the extent to which the projects have managed to become integrated into the daily life of the social welfare organizations and to have a future which extends beyond the pilot project period. Many factors seem to indicate that the projects had not become well integrated to any significant extent into current structures and practices, and that social work organizations have shown a tendency to be immune to changes. The most important effect which the evaluations highlight is the experience of the staff included in their projects, as these reforms have both increased staff know-how and preparedness to experiment, and promoted internal mobility of the staff members who have been very actively involved in the projects. In practice, the most positive result of this development of knowledge has been the experience obtained of social work in relation to groups of people and communities which have traditionally received assistance from the social welfare system. The ability to plan and implement projects targeted on specific problems and target groups has also been strengthened.

'Activation' measures in relation to young people

Before the completion of the SDF programme in 1991, other refrains than 'let all experimental projects flourish' were audible. Social policy discussion focused on how to 'activate' (encourage and include into society) the many unemployed people and marginalized people who were being passively supported – or, in other words, 'How is it possible to make rights and obligations walk hand in hand?'

Several activation programmes were initiated under slogans such as: 'From passive support to active measures' and 'Everybody is needed.' The activation strategy was presented politically as a completely new orientation in the field of Danish social policy. In recent years, this strategy has led to a number of changes in measures in relation to people who are in receipt of transfer payments – whether in the form of unemployment benefits or social assistance. As an element of the activation strategy, the Social Commission was set up in 1991 for the purpose of analysing the whole system of transfer payments and making proposals for a more forward-oriented, coherent and simplified system in which human and financial resources would be better utilized. The Social Commission has examined the conditions for different age groups. We will briefly describe some of the gloomy facts which were presented in 1992 regarding the situation of young people, and the changes in relation to the Social Assistance Act which have been introduced in relation to them.

The Social Commission has shown that not less than 75 per cent of all young persons receive cash assistance or unemployment benefit before they attain the age of 26 years. A closer look at this group shows that the proportion receiving assistance is 90 per cent for those groups of young persons who have only undergone basic compulsory schooling (10 years). Young people with only basic compulsory schooling are also the group with the longest contacts with the social security system, and up to 13 per cent of each generation of younger people are on public assistance for at least three years. As regards young immigrants, the picture is even more dismal, as 25 per cent of young immigrants are unemployed, and only 10 per cent have undergone qualifying education or training, whereas in other groups of young people, about 65 per cent undergo qualifying education or training.

The following examples of activation measures initiated in recent years for young people can be mentioned: an increase in the capacity of the educational/training system, differentiated wages, and work instead of social assistance. When a young person today contacts the social security office to apply for social assistance, he or she must be given an offer of employment within 14 days. The young person cannot refuse this 'offer' or the assistance will be withdrawn. The evaluations of this new 'workfare' policy which have been carried out to date seem to indicate that most young people are satisfied with the scheme. However, it is still premature to say whether the scheme will, to any significant extent, be able to keep the young in employment or encourage them to enter education or training.

Within the municipal social administrations, the scheme has led to organizational changes, with the establishment of special youth sections and employment offices to work in co-operation with the public employment services. Many social workers have become activation agents – this is highly desirable in relation to the many, especially young, people whose only problem is lack of work and education/training. However, there is a professional problem for many social workers working in these areas: resources are often used to provide jobs for those otherwise well-functioning young persons who are easily placed on the labour market, and this leaves fewer resources for the more disadvantaged groups of young people. Another professional problem for social workers is the concern that such a strong focus on employment/education and training ignores the need for broader and more personally-targeted initiatives in relation to more vulnerable young people – for instance young, single mothers, who are in many cases treated on an equal footing with other young people.

In relation to the education programme for social workers, the activation strategy has raised questions, such as whether there is a need for some form of specialization in social work concerning labour market/training issues, or whether the activation strategy should lead to an intensification of the education programme dealing with other difficulties which young persons experience, so as to ensure that the special needs of these vulnerable people are not ignored in the present climate.

Practice: Children and families

In recent years, children's living conditions, the social problems of families and children, and social work with children have been key themes in the fields of research, legislation and social education. There has been little co-ordination of activities in these different fields, but there is no doubt that social work with children has been given considerable attention. A critical discussion has taken place in recent years on the quality of this work, and there has been evidence of a wish to strengthen initiatives that help to prevent families finding themselves in situations that are damaging for their children. Also, there has been discussion of the need to help families deal more successfully with problematic situations when these have arisen.

Research concerning children has been a high priority at the largest research institution in the social sector in Denmark, the Socialforsknings-instituttet (Social Research Institute), and also among other researchers attached to universities and similar educational institutions. This means that valuable new research publications in this central field of social work are now available. Publications from the Social Research Institute include reports on: children placed in care outside their home (including analysis of repeated placements during childhood); disadvantaged families' own views of their situations; failure to care appropriately for children, and the circumstances of families where such neglect takes place; placements with foster families; the subsequent social situation of children who have been placed in care, and the quality of the work of the municipal social administrations in connection with placement of children outside their home. Publications from other educational institutions (including schools of social work) have been published during the same period. These reports have examined topics such as: children's personal experiences of the process of being placed in care; theories on risk and children; social work in Copenhagen in connection with compulsory placements in care outside the home; the social situation of single mothers and the possibilities for assisting them (a comparative study of three countries); how families experience their contacts with the social system, and several reports on the history and development of the child welfare services.

In the field of legislation, a committee set up to investigate the nature of social work of the municipal administrations with children and families submitted its report in 1990 (Socialministeriet, 1990). This report led to major changes in the Social Assistance Act regarding the rules on social work practice in relation to families and children, in particular the rules concerning placement of children in care outside the home. These came into operation on 1 January 1993. The primary objective of these legislative amendments has been to strengthen families' and children's legal rights in connection with placement in care. Decisions to take children into care are taken administratively, but the composition of the body which takes these decisions has been changed so that the legal and professional element has been strengthened. Another important element of these changes is that both parents and children above the age of 15 years are now considered actual parties to the case and may be given the right to independent and separate legal representation. The rules on informed consent have been changed to take into account, to a larger extent, the views of the parents and the children. Detailed procedural rules have been established for the investigation process, and requirements for the documentation of the child's and the family's situation are in force. Many social workers see these procedural rules as an instrument to strengthen the quality of the social work, as the rules are in the form of guidelines that promote a professional and methodological approach to practice.

However, the criteria determining a decision to place a child in care, with or without the consent of the parents, have not been changed in any significant way. These criteria, as laid down in the new Act, are still broad and give the authorities ample discretion to define the conditions which fall under these criteria. The rules do not in any way specify precisely what must be considered unacceptable living conditions for a child. Against this background, it remains an open question whether the new rules will offer families adequate legal protection. Procedural rules may be an important element in efforts to ensure proper legal administration, but they do not solve the most important problem in this field: how to define the concept of abuse and neglect of children, and in particular, when is neglect so serious that the public authorities must intervene?

As mentioned above, this Act has been in force for only a relatively short period, hence it is difficult to draw any firm conclusions about its effect. However, several municipal administrations, in respect of this difficult work with children and families, have chosen bureaucratic solutions to what the preparatory work to the legislation characterized as a professional problem. For example, some of these municipal administrations have produced a number of forms, and the completion of these forms satisfies the legal requirements of the process; however, these processes hardly live up to the intentions underlying the introduction of the new legislation.

In social work education – not least at post-graduate levels – a variety of new initiatives have been taken as a result of the new legislation, such as offering courses, consultancy activities and supervision with a view to strengthening social workers' skills through higher-level qualifications in this field. Many efforts have been made to develop knowledge and methods in this field of practice. There has been great interest and participation in these educational activities, and a willingness on the part of the employers to finance participation by staff in such educational activities.

Practice: Ethnic minorities and mentally ill people

There are two significant groups in Danish society for social work practice which will be considered briefly here: ethnic minorities and those with mental illness. Although no major new social policy developments have taken place in relation to these two groups in recent years, it is important to consider new initiatives that may have an impact on their situation.

In Denmark, 3–4 per cent of the population belong to groups of non-Danish origin and, as in many other European countries, society has been slow to recognize that ethnic minorities have become a permanent element of Danish life. However, this growing awareness of the multi-cultural nature of society has not led to a proper integration policy which aims to place Danish and foreign citizens on an equal footing and to compensate for economic, social and cultural inequalities.

In relation to mentally ill people, Denmark has experienced similar developments to many other parts of the Western world. Recent years have been characterized by the closure of large institutions, which should have been followed up by the development of locally-based initiatives to integrate mentally ill people into society. Some of these local support programmes have been established, for instance in the form of common housing facilities, but not to a sufficient extent and in sufficient numbers to satisfy all the needs of mentally ill people. In recent years, there has been some consideration of the re-establishment of places in institutions, but little has actually happened in this direction.

In the light of a growing concern that some residential quarters in large Danish cities are developing into 'social ghettos', the government has set up a City Committee which has put forward a major programme for the development of these social ghettos, and large funds have been earmarked for projects and developments in these areas. Indirectly, this may be important for both ethnic minorities and mentally ill people, because many of them are living in these deprived neighbourhoods along with other people who, for a variety of reasons, are receiving social assistance.

This City Programme has been formulated with 30 objectives which aim to create activities in urban areas, such as:

- strengthening social networks;
- initiating do-it-yourself work and neighbour support;
- strengthening co-operation among housing associations, the social sector, the Church and local associations;
- establishing more leisure-time activities for children and young people;
- offering financial assistance to municipalities with large ghettos, etc.

Some of these objectives are specifically targeted at ethnic minorities, and they take the form of both offers of assistance and restrictions in relation to them. There are various measures to support ethnic minorities: for example, to assist mothers and children to integrate into daycare facilities. Support is also given to firms run by immigrants if they offer training places/practical training to young immigrants. Other measures tighten the already strict rules for immigrants, and intensify social controls over these groups. As an example, municipal administrations have the right to refuse to offer housing to immigrants if there are already many immigrants in the residential area concerned. The authorities can take steps to ensure a more equal distribution of immigrant children in all the schools within the municipality. Furthermore, it is proposed to tighten the rules on family reunion so that it must be substantiated that the applicant is able to support the family; it is also proposed to offer financial assistance for repatriation, etc.

It is difficult to evaluate the consequences of this urban development work for the various groups in the local areas concerned. It is especially difficult because the programme is inconsistent, in that it mixes the development of some local areas with reductions in other areas of expenditure, restrictions on people, and increased social controls. However, the amount of financial resources earmarked for this purpose show that some action in this field is being taken. In relation to social work, these developments may mean a further strengthening of social work practice with groups, an increased focus on community development in co-operation with agencies in the private sector, and increased voluntary initiatives. In the educational field, this has already led to new initiatives in the form of the planning of educational activities for social work practitioners – mainly at the post-graduate level – with a view to strengthening the qualifications for these new tasks.

Organizational structures: The voluntary and private sector

As described above, the SDF programme, the activation strategy and the Social Commission all result from strong and widespread criticisms of the development of the social welfare state. This critical analysis also applies to a growing social policy interest in the voluntary and private sectors. Although the voluntary and private social sectors have a long tradition and history in Danish social welfare, until five or six years ago these sectors had been secluded from the expansion of the welfare state. However, criticism of the high cost of the welfare state, its patronizing role, excessive social control, and the rigid organizational structures and bureaucracy of social institutions has illuminated the potential role of the voluntary and private sectors as part of social welfare. The biggest problems in moving from a centrally-organized welfare state to a welfare society where the public sector and the private sector establish partnerships to prevent and solve social problems are:

- how to organize the division of labour;
- which sector is best able to provide which service;
- how to overcome the many myths and prejudices within these two sectors.

The voluntary and private sectors will benefit from having increased financial attention. However, at the same time they risk being overloaded by tasks because of limited personnel resources. They are also in danger of losing their special characteristics through increased state influence on voluntary work.

As a concrete result of the interest in strengthening the social voluntary and private sector, public funds were appropriated in 1992 for the establishment of a Centre for Voluntary Social Work. The objective of this organization is to promote and strengthen the development of voluntary social work in Denmark. To achieve this, the centre offers a broad range of services to the private sector in the form of consultancy and information activities. Hence, it promotes the development of knowledge and methodologies – not least in relation to models of co-operation between public administrations and voluntary organizations at the local level. In work towards the development of co-operation models, a barrier remains: many professionally-trained social workers in the public sector are reluctant and uncertain when it comes to the reality of establishing co-operation on a professional basis. In line with the increased inflow of public funds into the private sector, a greater number of social workers are now recruited in this sector. Their functions are typically broader than in the public sector, and they work as consultants, supervisors, initiators and organizers in areas such as self-help projects and voluntary placement activities.

The increased focus on the voluntary and private social sector has not yet had any major impact upon either basic or post-graduate education of social workers. At all levels of education, about two days are reserved for thematic education in co-operation with voluntary organizations. But the right model for this aspect of education for social work has not yet been found, partly because this is a difficult process – especially at the basic level – as students are seeking to develop a professional profile and identity, aimed, in particular, at professional social work with families within the framework of public social institutions and administrations, and also because a similar reluctance and uncertainty in relation to the voluntary and private sector (see above) can be found among teachers as well as among practitioners.

Major developments in social work education

The Danish system for the public education of social workers comprises five educational institutions (Copenhagen, Odense, Esbjerg, Århus, and Ålborg) which between them provide social work education at four levels.

1   *Basic education* – Basic education consists of a three- to three-and-a-half-year course where students are specifically trained in the theory and methodology of social work. On completion of this basic training, students qualify as a social worker and are deemed competent for recruitment and work in both public and private social institutions.[1]

[1] Administratively-trained staff may undergo a course of 800 hours at the Administration School, which will give them the same formal qualifications as the training offered by the five educational institutions mentioned.

2   *Post-graduate short courses* – Currently, these social work training schools offer a number of courses of differing length with a view to developing and updating the knowledge and skills of social workers. The content of these courses is, to a large extent, determined by the training needs arising in everyday social work practice as a consequence of the ongoing changes in social legislation and in the organization of the social welfare sector.

3   *One-year courses – the advanced social work studies programme* – This programme provides for post-graduate study of ten months' duration for social workers with at least five years' practical experience and 150 hours' post-graduate training. The content of the course focuses on advanced treatment methods, supervision, consultation, and evaluation methods. On completion of the programme, the participants receive a certificate, but it is not a degree which provides a right to occupy special positions in the employment hierarchy.

4   *The masters programme* – In 1992, a social education programme at masters level was introduced, as a pilot project in co-operation between the Schools for Training of Social Workers in Copenhagen and Ålborg University. This type of education has been evaluated, and the programme has become permanent. The admission criteria are completion of basic social work education and five years' practical social work. It is a part-time course (corresponding to half-time), which students follow for four years while they continue to work.

Evaluations of basic professional education

Until 1996, the content and form of basic social work education was based on a 1978 order issued by the Ministry for Education. Although this order leaves some opportunities for educational development within individual training institutions, in recent years there have been substantial calls (from both students and teachers) for a changed formal legal base to social work education, in the light of the many changes that have taken place in the social welfare field. These calls for change have been made with a view to obtaining a more solid and broad-based foundation for the future education of social workers. Two major evaluations of basic education have taken place since 1991 (Evalueringscenteret, 1994).

The main problems which both evaluation studies address are the need for:

●   the development of closer and more varied interaction between the theory and practice of social work;

- a higher priority for the professional content of social work education, including discussion of whether the generic content should be maintained, or whether some sort of specialization should take place at the level of basic education.

The training institutions tend to favour maintaining the generalist model, and wish to extend the course by 6–12 months. Such an extension would also make it possible for students to experience other forms of practical work experience than those allowed under the present structure, where practical experience only covers one term of the course.

The evaluations have led to changes in basic social work education (summer 1996). The changes are in line with the general trend in Denmark regarding the issuing of administrative orders in the educational field. Such orders tend to lay down the overall objectives and the broad framework for achieving these objectives – a far less detailed regulation than the present one. Also, the establishment of the masters programme will probably also have an impact upon the structure and content of future basic education.

Increase in the number of students

Following serious reductions in the number of places for students throughout the 1980s, in 1993 politicians decided to increase the number of places in the educational system significantly, and also within higher education. The decision was taken on the basis of documentation (for example, from the Social Commission mentioned above) showing a high level of unemployment and a shortage of education/training places for young people. Regarding education of social workers, this change increased the number of places in 1993–94, and at very short notice extended the numbers of social work students in individual institutions by 25–50 per cent. The financial implications of increased capacity within the educational system are difficult to calculate because the system of financing was changed at the same time as the increase in student numbers. However, in spite of many practical problems (for instance, shortage of teachers), this increase in the number of students was welcomed, both within and outside the education institutions. A number of regions in Denmark are suffering from a shortage of qualified social workers, following several years with a high level of unemployment for this group. Hence, an increase in the number of qualified social workers will be of considerable importance.

Developing the masters programme

This educational programme aims at further developing social workers' specialization in direct work with clients by giving participants qualifications to enable them to undertake research, social policy analyses, programme development, organizational analyses and structural changes in human service organizations. The masters programme is thus based on students' thorough knowledge and experience of practical social work, and against this background the programme aims to enable students to develop the frameworks for their work. During the first experimental years of this programme, the students admitted have primarily been in the older age group (average age about 40 years) with substantial experience in practical social work – some in senior and executive positions. Often, these social workers have passed the stage of life of being responsible for small children, and thus have a better chance of successfully completing the very demanding combination of study and work.

It is our hope that the masters programme will, through research, strengthen the development of qualifications in social work. There is a considerable amount of social research in Denmark, but until now only a small amount of research has been undertaken that illustrates the concrete realities of social work, the framework within which it is performed, and its effects and processes. A research-based development of knowledge and methods focusing on the central problems of practical social work will be the main objective of the masters programme.

Themes and issues

There is an important theme that is central to Danish social work education: the development of international approaches. The development of social work education in recent years has been characterized by growing international co-operation. All schools for social work training are involved in exchange programmes (for both students and teachers), mainly in connection with the ERASMUS (now SOCRATES) and Nordplus programmes. Some schools have set a target to ensure that within a few years all students will go on a study trip abroad as an element of their education, but other schools seem to find it difficult to combine a study trip of three months' duration (as required under these programmes) with the very tight daily timetable and the many examinations.

Another factor which tends to act as an obstacle to internationalization is the high average age of the students (about 30 years), as family responsibilities may prevent them from travelling abroad, or make it very difficult. Also, administrative tasks in connection with the planning and realization of study visits hinder this activity, as the schools of social work are relatively small educational institutions which find it difficult to make staff resources available for these tasks.

Endword

This brief survey of the present state of affairs and development trends in social policy, social work and social work education in Denmark seems to indicate that we are living in an era of dramatic changes. The values on which the social welfare model has been based are being questioned, objectives have changed, and experiments are being carried out within a more pluralistic welfare model. This will have significant implications for social work, which must function in the midst of this upheaval and yet at the same time undergo a process in which the impact of practice on target groups is re-evaluated as new working methods are developed and the quality of the social work is subjected to scrutiny and extensive debate.

In the field of education, we have seen major innovations – not least in the development of a masters programme – and in the coming years we will undoubtedly see many changes in the content and structure at all levels of education. But it is difficult to predict exactly in which directions the developments will take social work, as this upheaval process is characterized by so many opposing trends that it is not possible to forecast future developments with any reasonable degree of certainty.

3 Social work in Germany

David Kramer

Introduction

With nearly 80 million inhabitants, reunified Germany is the most populous country in the European Union. Beyond this, it combines an elaborate welfare state with a highly-developed form of federalism which allows and even encourages a good deal of diversity among the various *Länder* of the country. The act of reunification joined two former German states which in many ways were very different from each other. Although the West German legal and economic framework was adopted by the east, there are still many differences between the two components of reunified Germany. Thus it is often very difficult to make valid generalizations which apply to the country as a whole.

In compiling this chapter, I relied on available literature and on my own experience in social work education in Germany. In addition, I commissioned a survey of social work. I received about twenty responses from various schools, which helped to round out my impressions of the actual situation at German schools of social work. I have no illusions that the following report can claim to be comprehensive with respect to the complex questions it covers. It should, rather, be viewed as suggestive.

Reunified Germany has a highly-developed and well-designed welfare state which has survived two world wars, the Great Depression of the 1930s, the totalitarianism of the right from 1933 to 1945, the (nearly) total collapse of 1945, the totalitarianism of the left from 1945 to 1989 in the eastern parts of Germany, the (nearly) total collapse of the German Democratic Republic (GDR) in 1989–90, and reunification. The system is sturdy, although it will no doubt be obliged to make painful adjustments to demographic changes in German society. It is certainly no accident that capitalist welfare states around the world have patterned themselves to a considerable extent on the German model.

25

The roots of this welfare state extend deeply back into German/Prussian history. Not only was the most celebrated architect of the modern German welfare state, Otto von Bismarck, a self-proclaimed 'reactionary', many of his central notions were, in fact, anticipated by the Prussian historical experience (Habermann, 1994).

The modern welfare state in Germany is a product not only of Bismarck, but of social democrats, Nazis, Christian democrats and technocrats. The various elements can no longer be entirely distinguished, and they have been blended with elements of liberalism from the immediate post-Second World War period. The result, the social-market economy, is a 'model' which has admirers and detractors around the world. The German welfare state defines itself anew every day within the framework of German social development – but it does so on the basis of a logic which is polymorphic, even contra-dictory.

According to the Constitution of the Federal Republic of Germany, which was accepted by the former GDR in 1990, Germany is a democratic and *social* federal state. Two principles are in operation: solidarity and subsidiarity. Both the government and individual citizens have the responsibility to act in a spirit of social solidarity. Subsidiarity, as defined by the Federal Consti-tutional Court (the supreme court in the Federal Republic of Germany), means:

> that the community in the narrow sense should act first, and that the state should intervene only when there is no alternative. (Wienand, 1988, pp.8–9)

Social work practice in Germany

There are three 'pillars' of the social welfare system in Germany:

1   Social insurance;
2   Social maintenance and social equalization;
3   Welfare.

Social insurance is based on legal entitlements, is not means-tested, and is financed on a pay-as-you-go basis by contributions paid by employers and employees. *Social maintenance* and *social equalization* are paid for from state tax revenues on the basis of legal entitlements. *Welfare* is means-tested and is generally characterized by the principle of subsidiarity in relation to other benefit commitments (Wienand, 1988, pp.10–11). Legislation has now been introduced in parliament which would substantially reduce the influence of the 'subsidiarity principle' in the provision of welfare.

The German welfare state comprehends a complex interaction between federal legislation and state (*Länder*) or communal execution. Outside the areas of social insurance, the 'subsidiarity principle' has also traditionally subsumed the activity of umbrella organizations of 'private welfare'. These are:

- Workers' Welfare Association (Arbeiterwohlfahrt);
- Service Agency of the Protestant Church in Germany (Diakonisches Werk der Evangelischen Kirche in Deutschland);
- German Caritas Federation (Deutscher Caritasverband);
- German Non-denominational Welfare Association (Deutscher Paritätischer Wohlfahrtsverband);
- German Red Cross (Deutsches Rotes Kreuz);
- Central Welfare Office of the Jews in Germany (Zentralwohlfahrtsstelle der Juden in Deutschland) (Landwehr with Wolff, 1992, pp.17–19).

The large voluntary welfare agencies have together formed the Federal Association of Voluntary Welfare Agencies. All of the large voluntary welfare agencies are similar in that they have assumed certain of the state's obligations in the social sector. The voluntary agencies run a considerable number of services, facilities, homes, programmes and events. They receive public funds for their work, but they also contribute from their own resources, particularly from donations in money and kind. Unpaid voluntary work is a vital element for these associations (Wienand, 1988, pp.19–21).

With respect to working specifically with foreigners, the large private welfare agencies have adopted a division of labour which appears curious at first glance, but seems to work well in practice. The Workers' Welfare Association looks after persons from Turkey and the predominantly Islamic parts of the former Yugoslavia. The Service Agency of the Protestant Church in Germany attends primarily to persons from Greece and to other non-Catholics from dominantly Christian areas. The German Caritas Federation works primarily with persons from Catholic countries or the Catholic parts of the former Yugoslavia. The large private welfare agencies and some governmental agencies employ Social Counsellors for Foreign Workers and their Families. Such counsellors are generally members of ethnic minorities. Twice, beginning in 1986 and 1991, the Alice-Salomon-Fachhochschule Berlin conducted intensive two-year courses to provide further qualifications for such counsellors. The courses led to certification, but not to a diploma in social work.

A useful compendium of information on social work with, by and for migrants and ethnic minorities in Germany has been produced by the Institut für Sozialarbeit und Sozialpädagogik[1]. The compendium, which is published

---

[1] Contact address: Am Stockborn 5–7, 60439 Frankfurt am Main, Germany.

three times a year, is invaluable for anyone trying to grasp the many problems connected with migration and ethnicity, and their implications for social work in Germany (cf. Institut für Sozialarbeit und Sozialpädagogik, 1994).

The variety of social service provision at the local level is well illustrated by former West Berlin. Prior to the political upheaval of 1989–90, West Berlin had over 4,000 organizations, institutions and agencies involved in offering social services of the most diverse nature (Kramer and Landwehr, 1988). That number, of course, is much larger today, due to the expansion of the system to include former East Berlin.

There are about 130,000 persons in Germany with a formal qualification in social work. Of these, over two-thirds are women. Approximately 86,000 persons with formal social work qualifications are currently employed. During the 1980s, many social workers experienced difficulty in finding jobs. Unemployment rose from 4,000 in 1980 to 12,000 in 1988. However, by 1991 the number of unemployed had fallen to 7,400. At present, the job prospects of social workers appear to be no worse – and perhaps are even better – than most other professions represented at *Fachhochschulen* (Bausch, 1995, pp.26, 31–2). Professional social workers constitute, to a very considerable degree, the middle management of the German welfare state. There is currently much discussion about whether their prospects on the labour market are better or worse than other levels of middle management.

Social work education in Germany

The basic design of social work education in Germany has changed remarkably little since 1986, when it was described in some detail by Baron et al. (1986). Of course, German reunification in 1990 affected social work education, in that it extended the prevailing system in former West Germany to the territory of the former GDR, but the fundamental features of the system remained largely intact.

The beginnings of education in the social professions in Germany can be traced back to the first courses of the Girls' and Women's Groups for Social Assistance Work, founded in Berlin in 1893 by Jeanette Schwerin and the German Society for Ethical Culture. In 1899, a one-year training programme was established under the direction of Alice Salomon. In 1905, the Protestant Church in Hanover founded the first real Women's School for Social Welfare. In 1908, Alice Salomon opened the first women's social school with a two-year programme in Berlin – a programme which was soon to be emulated all over Germany.

For various reasons, social work education in Germany was established both outside the university system and below the level of universities within the German educational hierarchy. This pattern has persisted until the present day.

During the Nazi period, social work practice and social work education were purged of 'racial' and political 'undesirables' and, in general, were debased by Nazi ideology (Kramer, 1983a). As early as 1933, Alice Salomon was removed from the school she had founded and from all official offices in Germany; in 1937 she was expelled from the country (Salomon, 1983, p.8; Wieler, 1987). However, at the same time that the Nazis were shaping social work education for their own purposes, they did make some gestures towards an improvement in the formal status of social work education (Kramer, 1983b, pp.53–7).

After the collapse of the Third Reich in 1945, democratized schools of social work were established in the western areas of Germany and West Berlin. Although after the Second World War more and more of the former women's schools began to admit men, social work continued to be overwhelmingly a 'female' occupation. Even at present, approximately two-thirds of the students of social work are women (Bausch, 1995, p.29).

Not until the late 1960s were undergraduate courses of social pedagogy established in the departments of education at certain German universities (their precursors at the universities of Frankfurt am Main and Jena and at the German Academy for Social and Pedagogical Women's Work had not survived the Nazi period). Graduates of university courses are not eligible for state licensing as professional social workers.

In 1970–71, non-university programmes of social work education, along with certain other programmes in business, engineering and administration, all of which had previously belonged to secondary education, were transformed into colleges (*Fachhochschulen*) and were integrated into the system of higher education. *Fachhochschulen* are supposed to provide practice-oriented courses of study 'on a scientific basis' through an academic faculty. The desire to provide a 'scientific' foundation for social work encountered criticism from employers, who, for reasons of status, salary expectations and qualification, rejected the idea of academically-trained social workers as being too far removed from the reality of social work practice.

The GDR, largely for ideological reasons, rejected the profession of social work, although it did have social services, and even something very much like social work professionals; however, different structures and designations were used. Education for quasi-social work professionals in the GDR was non-generic, and in some areas highly specialized. East German qualifications in quasi-social work have not been recognized in reunified Germany as equivalent to professional social work qualifications. In the first years after reunification, a number of private institutions offered 'bridge-courses' which were advertised as opening the door to state licensing for professionals who had earned their qualification in the GDR. Such licensing has not been

forthcoming, and much controversy has developed about the quality of
many of the 'bridge-courses' (Bausch, 1995, pp.25–6). Some of the new
schools (or departments) of social work in the eastern parts of reunified Germany offer the possibility of an external examination for social work
professionals whose qualifications are not recognized. The Alice-Salomon-
Fachhochschule Berlin (located in what was formerly West Berlin) took the
lead in developing a compact course of studies for professionals from East
Berlin and East Germany in co-operation with a private institution in East
Berlin, the Förderverein für Jugend-und-Sozialarbeit. This pioneering programme opened the way to a recognized diploma and full state licensing for
professionals from East Germany. Roughly similar programmes have since
been implemented at the *Fachhochschulen* in Zittau-Görlitz, Magdeburg,
Merseburg and Potsdam.

Meanwhile, even before reunification, another type of social work education leading to state licensing had emerged in parts of Germany: professional
academies (*Berufsakademien*). There was – and still is – much controversy
about this form of professional training, since it is viewed by many as not
meeting the minimal academic standards of higher education.

There are 82 schools of social work in reunified Germany. Most of the
schools (or departments) of social work at the *Fachhochschule* level belong to
an organization called the FBT (Fachbereichstag Soziale Arbeit)[1]. The FBT
presently has 70 member institutions offering degrees in social work
(*Sozialarbeit*), social pedagogy (*Sozialpädagogik*) or social affairs (*Sozialwesen*).
The differences between the training leading to the three types of degree are
not great: often applications from all three types of degree-holders are
accepted for the same jobs. Traditionally, social work is thought to be
oriented more strongly towards administrative tasks in agencies; social
pedagogy is thought to be more strongly oriented towards areas like
youth and community work and to counselling, and social affairs is some
mysterious combination of both.

There is great diversity among the schools and departments of social work
throughout Germany. Some are affiliated to Churches, some are independent
schools (with or without various social work-related departments), some are
departments in larger *Fachhochschulen*. Some schools are quite large, with student bodies substantially exceeding 1,000; others are very small, with about
100 students in all. The average size seems to be about 400–500 students. In
all, there are approximately 40,000 students of social work, social pedagogy
and social affairs at German *Fachhochschulen*. About 6,700 new graduates
enter the workforce each year (Bausch, 1995, p.29).

The organization of study falls into two basic patterns:

[1] The FBT was previously known by the initials KFS.

1 Six or seven semesters of study, including at least one semester of supervised fieldwork, leading to a diploma, followed by a year of professional internship and state licensing – this is the *two-phase model*, prevalent in northern Germany;

2 Eight semesters of studies, including two semesters of supervised fieldwork, leading to a diploma and state licensing – this is the *one-phase model*, prevalent in southern Germany. (To confuse matters further: the *Land* of Hessia, in the middle of Germany, operates both models.)

With varying focuses and different ways of integrating fieldwork, the following areas of knowledge tend to be covered in courses of social work education:

● social work and social pedagogy – history, theories, organization and institutions, methods;

● social sciences – sociology, social policy, political science, economics, statistics, empirical social research;

● psychology/pedagogy – developmental psychology, therapeutic methods, theory and practice of education, theories of socialization;

● health – healthcare delivery, institutional and legal framework, medical surveys;

● law and public administration – legislation concerning family, youth, social welfare, social insurance, labour and administration;

● creative media and sports – music, drama, arts, film, video, handicrafts and sports.

Social work training is supposed to be generic rather than specialized (although, in reality, there are also countervailing tendencies at work). Many study programmes include courses in languages like English, Spanish and French. Schools with a focus on work with immigrants in particular tend to offer courses in the main immigrant languages. Some schools also offer courses in German for non-native German-speakers. At Church-affiliated schools, social ethics and social philosophy are usually included in the curricula. Some schools have a 'European' focus – sometimes even featuring periods of study or field placements in foreign countries (cf. Fachhochschule Frankfurt am Main, 1994).

Training during the early semesters generally concentrates on the introduction of basic knowledge in various social sciences, the legal framework, and basic theories and methods of social work. At many schools, the students have to pass an examination before they can continue the training. At most schools, the second part of the study programme allows students to choose among different focuses according to client groups, particular social problems, areas of social work and/or methods. Students must prepare and defend a substantial thesis (*Diplomarbeit*) in their area of specialization, and usually participate in 'projects'.

Universities and *Fachhochschulen* in Germany enjoy a high degree of constitutionally-guaranteed autonomy. Within the legal framework, they decide autonomously on all academic affairs: study programmes, examinations, curricula and admissions. They put forward names of professors, who are then hired by government, and they decide on hiring part-time teaching staff. Therefore, each department is autonomous in developing study programmes in social work as well as in other fields, and programmes and curricula vary greatly from school to school. There is no effective external control, co-ordination or accreditation on a national level. However, within the parameters of a federal system, efforts are being made to achieve a greater degree of co-ordination in social work education. Aside from the purely voluntary work of the FBT, which is based on the principle of consensus, a Commission for the Co-ordination of Curricula and Examinations in the area of education for social professions has been established by the Secretariat of the Standing Conference of Ministers of Culture in the Federal Republic of Germany.

Universities and *Fachhochschulen* are corporations of public law. All members – faculty, students, administrators – are represented in all important decision-making bodies of these institutions. The structure and composition of the bodies is regulated by federal and state law. As a rule, in all important matters the tenured faculty has the majority of votes, but the students are rather influential as well. Deans, chairpersons and presidents are elected from the tenured faculty.

State (*Länder*) ministries of science and universities oversee the higher education institutions within the legal framework. They are guided by legislation in dealing with academic affairs. The government has considerable influence in financial matters and in the appointment of tenured professors. Professors are civil servants, and are appointed for life.

A major problem in social work education in Germany is that *Fachhochschulen* are not allowed to grant the advanced degrees which, as a rule, are a prerequisite for full-time teaching positions at *Fachhochschulen*. This does not matter very much in subjects which are taught on a more or less competitive basis at both *Fachhochschulen* and universities. However, in the field of social work, this peculiar arrangement means that a graduate of a university course in social work cannot be a licensed social worker, while a graduate of a *Fachhochschule* cannot (as a rule) be hired as a professor of social work at a *Fachhochschule*.

There are provisions for extraordinary graduates from *Fachhochschulen* to continue their studies at a university for advanced degrees, and there are schemes for co-operative doctoral committees, although these tend to discriminate in various ways against the professors from *Fachhochschulen* (Keller, 1994).

There is currently a good deal of discussion at schools of social work and in the FBT concerning the need to establish a 'science of social work'. However, there is still a lack of clarity as to what precisely the defining characteristics of such a 'science' should be. The vast majority of tenured faculty at the schools of social work represent fields other than social work. Research at *Fachhochschulen* – although improving – is still underdeveloped and is officially subordinated to teaching. The requirement (in general) that professors at *Fachhochschulen* carry a teaching load of 18 contact hours per week is a major impediment to the development of social work research.

Higher education is provided without tuition fees in Germany. In theory, this opens the *Fachhochschulen* to less privileged sectors of the population. However, since there is a much stronger demand for places at schools of social work than can be met with the resources available, a very strict quota system for places applies. The results of this are that the state schools of social work have almost no control over admissions policy, which is conducted according to bureaucratic guidelines based primarily on secondary school grades and waiting periods. Church-affiliated schools have somewhat more influence over admissions, but they too are subject to outside meddling which has little to do with the best interests of a profession like social work. The bureaucratization of admissions policy makes it difficult for the individual schools to adopt flexible policies sensitive to the needs of minority and foreign communities resident in Germany. Since the children of foreign residents of Germany usually do not do as well in secondary school as the best German students, a quota system works to their disadvantage and makes it difficult for the schools of social work to achieve the degree of ethnic diversity which most of them would prefer. The bureaucratization of admissions policy is enforced by the courts and has encouraged a chain reaction of bureaucratization within the schools of social work which is seriously inhibiting their creativity and flexibility.

A survey of curricula carried out in late 1994 (Jörg, 1994) examined 62 formal curricula (*Studienordnungen*) of various departments and schools of social work at the *Fachhochschule* level. Of these 62 curricula, 22 were from Church-affiliated departments or schools (11 Catholic and 11 Protestant) and 11 were from schools or departments located in what was formerly East Germany (two of the curricula from the east were from Church-affiliated institutions). The data are summarized in Table 3.1.

The survey was a quantitative analysis of course content. The extent to which courses provided teaching about three key elements – ethnic and religious minorities, migration and human rights – was explored (see Table 3.2). Specifically, courses were asked to identify the number and nature of schools or departments that have these curriculum elements.

The survey showed that 25 of the 62 curricula (40.3 per cent) contained positive indicators in respect of the three curriculum elements. Of these 25

Table 3.1   Details of institutions surveyed

	Absolute numbers	Percentages
Schools and departments	62	100
Church-affiliated institutions	22	35.5
– Protestant	11	17.75
– Catholic	11	17.75
Schools and departments located in former E. Germany	9	14.51
– Church-affiliated institutions in E. Germany	2	3.2
(Catholic/Protestant)	(1/1)	(1.6/1.6)

Table 3.2   Curricula with positive analytic indicators in respect of the three elements

	Absolute numbers	Percentages
Curricula	25	40.3
Church-affiliated institutions	8	36.4
– Protestant	1	9.1
– Catholic	7	63.6
Institutions in E. Germany	7	77.7
Church-affiliated institutions in E. Germany	1	50.0
(Catholic/Protestant)	(1/0)	(100/0)

schools/departments, eight were from Church-affiliated institutions. Catholic institutions predominated, with a total of seven. Furthermore, seven positive indicators were also identified in curricula from institutions located in former East Germany. Positive indicators were identified in the curriculum of one Catholic *Fachhochschule* in the east.

Positive indicators of these elements were not identified in a majority of the curricula of German schools and departments of social work surveyed. Only 40.3 per cent had curricular elements which could be so identified. On the other hand, it is noteworthy that the newly-founded schools and departments of social work in the east have a much better percentage than the schools located in what was formerly West Germany: 77.7 per cent of the schools/departments in the east have positive indicators in their curriculum for at least one of the elements which were surveyed, and this trend finds confirmation in each of the discrete categories. With respect to *ethnic and religious minorities*, the study also indicated that the percentage of curricula in which positive indicators could be identified was 27.7 per cent for the west and 42.9 per cent for the east; with respect to *migration*, the percentage was 50 per cent for the west and 57.1 per cent for the east; with respect to *human rights*, the percentage was 38.8 per cent for the west and 42.9 per cent for the east. It is also noteworthy that schools or departments with a Catholic affiliation are strongly represented in all analytic categories, but especially in the category 'human rights'.

In reality, the epistemological value of this survey is circumscribed by the very diversity of social work education in Germany. There are many efforts by schools/departments of social work, or by individuals associated with such institutions, to deal with the analytic categories relevant to this report which are not reflected in the survey of curricula (some of these will be cited below). That having been stipulated, however, there is still reason to believe that the newly-founded schools of social work in the east of reunified Germany may have an advantage of modernization with respect to their curricula in the analytical categories relevant to this report. The impressive showing of the Catholic schools/departments with respect to the analytical categories raises a number of questions that I will not pursue here, except to note that modernization and tradition may not always be as antithetical as is sometimes assumed.

The response to my appeal for information to the member institutions of the FBT in many cases confirmed Jörg's 1994 survey, but it also drew attention to the fact that not all of the relevant initiatives in social work education and practice relating to the analytical categories at issue in this report can be identified in curricula. I received over twenty responses to my letter to the 70 schools/departments of social work which are members of the FBT. It is not feasible to report here on all of the initiatives which were reported at the various *Fachhochschulen* in Germany. For the record, it should be noted that there are numerous relevant projects and initiatives in the following areas:

- research and project evaluation;
- practical projects and study projects;
- international co-operation (through ERASMUS and other European networks, but also on a bilateral level);

- conferences;
- fieldwork;
- student diploma papers;
- the real content of both standard and specialized course offerings.

The conclusion I reach is that there is much more concern and activity about questions concerning minorities, migration and human rights at German schools of social work than is readily visible. The challenge for the future is to make these activities more visible, to co-ordinate and disseminate them more effectively, and to evaluate them more systematically.

Nursing/nursing management: A new direction for German schools of social work

In recent years, numerous degree programmes in nursing or nursing management have been established by German schools of social work at the *Fachhochschule* level. Among the schools now offering such courses are: the Catholic FH Freiburg, the Catholic FH Munich, the Evangelical FH Berlin, the ASFH Berlin, the Hochschule Bremen, the FH Hamburg, the Evangelical FH Darmstadt, the FH Frankfurt, the FH Fulda, the FH Neubrandenburg, the FH Nordostniedersachsen (Lüneburg), the Catholic FH Norddeutschland (Osnabrück), the FH Osnabrück, the Evangelical FH Rheinland/Westfalen-Lippe (Bochum), the FH Bielefeld, the FH Münster, the Evangelical FH Ludwigshafen am Rhein, the Catholic FH Mainz and the FH Magdeburg.

The courses in nursing or nursing management are separate from the courses in social work. They correspond to a perceived need to enhance the professional competence and status of nursing personnel and open up possibilities of professional advancement for them. Due primarily to poor working conditions, low prestige and insufficient opportunities for advancement, it has been very difficult in recent years to keep qualified personnel in the nursing field. It is hoped that the courses will help to alleviate this and will enable nursing managers to take their rightful place of co-leadership in the healthcare delivery system.

Many of the courses in nursing or nursing management are designed for people working full-time or nearly full-time. This is an innovation which is not necessarily easy to arrange in the German system. Experience gained through these courses may facilitate more part-time courses of study in social work (and other fields) as well.

The question of why courses on nursing/nursing management are being offered by schools of social work is often raised. There are probably many partial answers to the question, but it is presumably relevant, in the German context, that nursing, like social work, is both a predominately female profession and one which is located on the border between the private and public spheres.

Changes in the financing and governance of the healthcare delivery system which are either being discussed or have already been adopted seem to be moving nursing in the direction of a market-driven profession. Questions of cost-efficiency and organization seem to be increasing in importance. Many observers feel that similar pressures will also be felt increasingly in the domains of classical social work. Thus, many German schools of social work believe that their experimentation with courses in nursing/nursing management are directly relevant for the further development of their social work courses as well.

Themes and issues: Problems and observations

Reunified Germany is confronted with a multi-faceted challenge: to integrate the two halves of a German nation which were divided by the Cold War; to arrange its affairs with its European neighbours; to find a way to accommodate migrants from cultures which are very different from the German; to modify and apply humanely the legal framework which has evolved from German history; to assume the leadership role which is expected of a large and wealthy country without exacerbating fears of German 'domination' in Europe, and to atone for German errors in the past without neglecting the feeling on the part of a significant portion of the German population that injustice was also experienced by many ethnic Germans in Eastern and South-eastern Europe in the post-Second World War period. None of this is easy.

On the other hand, the decentralization which is characteristic of German federalism makes it difficult to focus energies and resources. Schools/departments of social work have a high level of autonomy, yet there is much evidence that they are doing more than immediately meets the eye to prepare the profession of social work to confront the challenges of migration, minorities and the enforcement of human rights.

Endword

The German welfare state, though facing many problems of finance and design, has proven to be a very durable and flexible instrument. It is difficult to believe that the problems of tomorrow will be more intractable than those surmounted during the last hundred years.

With respect to questions concerning migration, minority issues and human rights, it is pertinent to point out that German social work and social work education have been far from inactive, but they still have a long way to go towards meeting the challenges of post-Communist Europe.

Acknowledgements

This chapter is based to a considerable degree upon a report submitted by the author to the Council of Europe's *1994/1995 Co-ordinated Research Programme in the Social Field: 'the initial and further training of social workers taking into account their changing role'*.

I am grateful to several colleagues at the Alice-Salomon-Fachhochschule Berlin who helped me in various ways to prepare this chapter. Particular thanks are due to Christine Labonté-Roset, the Rector of the ASFH, Klaus Johannssen, the Chancellor of the ASFH, Ingrid Kollak, professor on the Nursing Management course of the ASFH, Beate Pätsch, Günter Pirringer, Dorothea Salje and Rolf Landwehr from the administration of the ASFH, and, of course, to Lutz von Werder and Peter Jörg of the HDZ.

4 Social work in Ireland

Ann Lavan

Introduction

An emphasis on child protection and child care, an aspiration to develop family support services and a commitment to the appointment of more social workers is perhaps the clearest statement of contemporary issues in Irish social work. The impact of three child care inquiry reports – the Report of the Kilkenny Incest Inquiry (McGuinness, 1993), the Report on the death of Kelly Fitzgerald (Ireland, 1996a) and the Report into the Operation of Madonna House (Ireland, 1996b) – provoked renewed concern on the status of child care and repeated calls for full implementation of the 1991 Child Care Act. Between 1993 and the end of 1996, 900 new permanent posts were created in the Irish Child Care Services. These included 315 social work appointments, increasing the number of social workers in this sector by approximately one third. The 1991 Child Care Act was enacted against a background of emerging incidences of child abuse and imposes a clear statutory duty on health boards to provide a range of child care and family support services. While social workers are employed in other sectors – hospitals, local authorities, probation and welfare, semi-state organizations and a range of voluntary organizations – the majority of those employed in the health sector are involved in child care and child protection services. Issues concerning children and families are the paramount concern in Irish social work. The identification of social work with child care is deeply rooted in the antecedents of social work in Ireland, but the emphasis on child care has been intensified due to public disquiet arising from media attention surrounding the above reports.

Ireland in context

The 1980s saw the beginning of a time of rapid social change in Ireland, that continues today. In particular it has been a time of enormous changes in social legislation with the consequent implications for individuals, social relationships and families. Debates about abortion (arising out of the 'X' case) led to a referendum and subsequent legislation: the Regulation of Information (Services Outside the State for the Termination of Pregnancies) Act 1995. The Act sets out the conditions under which certain information about abortion services *outside* the state may be made available. The substantive issue of abortion within the state arising from the 'X' case remains. A referendum on divorce (the second in ten years) was held in November 1995. By the slimmest majority (fewer than 9,000 votes separating the 'yes' and 'no' votes), the Irish people favoured legalizing divorce. In drafting the wording of the amendment to the constitution, the government set out the grounds on which a court could dissolve a marriage.

Increasingly, the nature and role of the family is being placed under the spotlight: there has been a rapid increase in the number of births outside marriage; there are increasing numbers of women reporting violence in the home; instances of marital breakdown are on the increase. Whilst the Catholic Church continues to be significant for most people, the legitimacy of the Church's role as teacher and guardian of moral behaviour was called into sharp focus following revelations that have associated a number of priests with child sex abuse. Early in 1996, the Irish Catholic Bishops reported on the outcome of the deliberations of a broadly-based advisory committee which met over a period of two years and formulated a comprehensive set of guidelines on the issue of child sexual abuse by priests.

Arising out of the United Nations Year of the Family (1994), the government established a commission on the family in 1995. In an Interim Report published in 1996 entitled *Strengthening Families for Life*, the commission put forward six 'principles' which, it suggested, should guide family policy. These include: recognition that the family unit is a fundamental unit providing stability and well-being for our society; the unique and essential family function is that of caring and nurturing for all its members; continuity and stability are major requirements in family relationships; an equality of well-being is recognized between individual family members; family membership confers rights, duties and responsibilities; a diversity of family forms and relationships should be recognized (Ireland, 1996c).

Employment in Ireland

Ireland has a small (less than four million), relatively young, population. Almost half the population (44 per cent) is under the age of 25. Ten years ago Ireland had one of the highest unemployment rates in Europe. Now big companies are vying to attract young graduates and the 'Celtic Tiger' economy is booming. For years the average Irish worker had to support a high number of dependents, because of emigration in the 1950s, and in later years because of a large number of children and high unemployment. Now the baby boom children are entering the labour force and, unlike elsewhere in Europe, there will be no substantial pick-up in the number of old people as a percentage of population until 2010. Unemployment is expected to fall with the rate dropping from 12 per cent to 8.6 per cent by the year 2000. The Medium Term Review 1997–2003, published by the Economic and Social Research Institute, warns that the problem of long-term unemployment remains to be tackled and those with very limited education are likely to remain seriously disadvantaged (Duffy et al., 1997). Regional differences in unemployment are an ongoing concern with rates of unemployment being higher in certain rural and disadvantaged urban areas. Unemployment figures, in fact, mask huge regional differences with rates of unemployment being extremely high in certain parts of rural Ireland (O'Connor, 1991). A particularly worrying aspect of Irish unemployment is its long-term nature (O'Hearn, 1995). Despite the buoyant economy, concerns surrounding poverty and social exclusion remain a serious challenge facing Irish society (Curtin et al., 1996). Ensuring that the impact of rapid economic, social and demographic change does not increase social inequalities and social polarization is a key issue for those involved in setting the social policy agenda in Ireland. At the UN World Summit in Copenhagen, in March 1995, the Irish government endorsed a programme of action aimed at not only eliminating absolute poverty in the developing world but also reducing poverty and inequalities everywhere. Arising from this commitment, the government approved the development of a national anti-poverty strategy (NAPS), by an inter-departmental policy committee. In addition, the government made adoption and implementation of the NAPS a central feature of Partnership 2000 (Ireland, 1996d).

Practice: Social work and child care

In April 1994, the Minister for Health published a 'strategy for effective healthcare in the 1990s' entitled *Shaping a Healthier Future*, which contains a section devoted to 'Child care and family support services' (Department of Health, 1994). The emphasis on child care has been intensified due to the increase in numbers of reported and confirmed child abuse cases, and within this category, the numbers of confirmed cases involving sexual abuse. In 1983, there were 156 confirmed cases of child abuse. By 1986, the number of reports of alleged abuse received by health boards was just under 1,000. In almost 500 of these cases the abuse was confirmed, including 274 cases of child sexual abuse (Department of Health, 1994). The latest figures available indicate that in 1994 health boards received reports of more than 5,000 cases of child abuse (5,152) of which a little over 1,800 (1,869) cases were confirmed. In 1995, there were over 6,000 cases (6,415) reported to health boards, of which more than 2,000 (2,276) cases were confirmed. These included cases of physical, sexual, emotional abuse and neglect. The numbers of children in care have grown in both relative and absolute terms. At any one time almost 3,000 children are in the care of the health boards because their parents are under stress and unable to cope, and some due to child abuse and neglect (Department of Health, 1997a). The number of children in care on a compulsory basis has also increased, as has those in the care of foster families. The marked change in the way child care is developing is well illustrated by an examination of statistics for children in care. In 1970 the numbers of children in *residential* care was in the region of 3,700, while the figure for 1995 is about 750. In 1970, those who were fostered (boarded out) was approximately 1,300 while in 1995 that figure is estimated at 2,500 (McCabe, 1996).

The formation of the Irish Association of Social Workers in 1971 provided a new forum to join the strong lobby that had emerged in the 1960s, calling for new legislation (to replace the 1908 Children Act) and for improvements in child care services. In analysis of the contents of *The Irish Social Worker*, it was revealed that between 1980 and 1994 child care was a central concern of Irish social workers (Horgan, 1996). The purpose of the long-awaited 1991 Child Care Act was to update the law in relation to the care of children, particularly children who have been assaulted, ill-treated, neglected, sexually abused or who are at risk. As already indicated, up to the early 1970s the main statutory means of dealing with (deprived) children was to place them in residential care. This residential provision was almost entirely located in the voluntary sector and almost completely in the hands of religious organizations.

The main elements of the 1991 Child Care Act

1   The Act provides for a comprehensive and radical reform of the law in relation to the care and protection of children.
2   There is a clear statement concerning the statutory duty of health boards to promote the welfare of children, and to provide a range of child care and family support services. This represents a move in the philosophy of service provision and delivery from one of discretion and favour to one of rights and justice.
3   The definition of 'child', and thus the health boards' responsibilities, is extended to cover 16- to 18-year-olds.
4   There is an emphasis on partnership between health boards and community-based voluntary groups. Health boards are given the authority to make arrangements for voluntary groups to provide services on their behalf.

5   The guiding principle of the Act is that, while having regard to the rights and duties of parents, the welfare of the child is paramount.
6   The main aim of the Act is to enable children to remain with their own families wherever possible, or to be placed with extended family members should removal from parents be unavoidable.
7   There is an emphasis on the responsibilities of the parents and their role as partners with the other involved bodies. Such responsibility is to be emphasized even when children are taken into care, where access for parents and extended family members should be facilitated.
8   Health boards may obtain Supervision Orders which, for the first time, give them a legal right to visit a child at home.
9   The Act introduces systems for the inspection and supervision of pre-school services.
10 There is provision for the registration and inspection of children's residential centres.

The implementation of the 1991 Child Care Act

The Act had a lengthy and troubled history, and was eagerly anticipated by child care practitioners. It was not calculations by academics or indeed the long-standing child care lobby which spurred the government into providing more resources and speeding up the implementation of the Act. Rather it was media revelations about a case of a father charged with the rape, incest and assault of his daughter over a fifteen-year period between 1976 and 1991, and the subsequent inquiry into the case highlighting the extent of the problem of child abuse in Ireland, that provided the impetus for government action. The case, which became known as the Kilkenny Incest Case, shocked the Irish public, especially when it emerged that the victim had a number of contacts with a range of professionals during the fifteen-year period of abuse, but no action had been taken. The Kilkenny Incest Investigation (McGuinness, 1993), whose brief was 'to make recommendations for the future investiga-tion and management by the health services of cases of suspected child abuse' (p.11), was unique in that it was the first independent inquiry of its kind in Ireland. The Report of the Inquiry has had immense influence in the field of child care and child protection in terms of both policy and practice. Some of the key recommendations are listed below.

● Full implementation of the 1991 Child Care Act.
● The amendment of Articles 41 and 42 of the Irish Constitution, which refer to the rights of parents and the authority vested in the family, so as to include a statement on the constitutional rights of children.
● To overhaul the existing Child Abuse Guidelines to include and to develop:

- a mandatory system of reporting suspected cases of abuse;
- written protocols on inter-professional and inter-agency collaboration.

The report particularly recognized the importance of liaison between health boards and the *gardai* (police). It recommended the establishment of formal policies and protocols to ensure greater clarity and agreement, as well as the provision of specialist officers and the introduction of joint training. The report also identified a key role for managers, whose role in the Irish health and social services system it highlighted as not fully developed during the history of the Kilkenny case. It was recommended that health board managers should take responsibility for ensuring that inter-agency reviews were carried out; and recommended a protocol for the maintenance of a Child Abuse Register; and a protocol for the conducting of case conferences, which the report saw as playing a pivotal role in encouraging interdisciplinary contact and parental involvement.

Impact of the Kilkenny incest investigation

The Report of the Kilkenny Inquiry (South Eastern Health Board, 1993) was praised in all quarters. It succeeded in clarifying the issues surrounding child abuse for social workers, parents and children. In particular, it was praised for not simply looking for scapegoats, either at an individual or professional level; rather, the report ensured that attention was focused on a much-needed debate covering the whole of the child care system in Ireland. The report was seen by all as succeeding in highlighting child abuse as a major social problem, and being crucial in reformulating social work policy and practice in Ireland. By implication, it highlighted the need for professionals to be more proactive on behalf of abused children, to be more child/victim-centred, and it drew attention to the need for professionals to work together and, more importantly, to develop a clearer understanding of what they should be working together *for*.

Issues arising from the 1991 Child Care Act: Research, policy and practice

The research carried out by McKeown et al. (1991), involving a statistical analysis of all suspected and confirmed abuse cases known to social workers in the ten community care areas of the Eastern Health Boards in 1988, was a significant milestone in the research literature. It provided important evidence of the number of cases of abuse, the patterns and effects of abuse, and the patterns and effects of professional intervention. However, in general, research into the causes and the nature of child abuse in Ireland has been largely conspicuous by its absence. Duggan notes that there has been a dearth of empirical and conceptual research undertaken in Ireland, and much of what has now been enacted in the 1991 Child Care Act, he suggests, is based on speculative information (Duggan, 1991, p.12). There are also problems around the dissemination of research, as there is no clear profile of the nature and extent of research which may be ongoing. There are also problems arising from the almost complete absence of reliable statistics from official sources. However, it was the intense media attention given to high-profile abuse cases, and the resulting increased public awareness and public pressure for action, which focused the debate on the need for change and the development of good practice, rather than empirical research findings.

The need to develop an integrated system of child care services

A major concern in child care literature is that in contemporary Ireland there is a tendency to equate child care with child protection. For example, in *On Behalf of the Child* (Ferguson and Kenny, 1995), contributors to the book stress that child protection is only part of a range of services which need to be developed and that an integrated system of child care services, backed up by adequate resourcing, needs to be introduced, particularly to facilitate the provision of more preventive services. Kilmurray and Richardson (1994) note that in reality, the services provided have, through public pressure, professional direction and lack of resources, developed along a crisis-intervention model, reacting to suspected or known abuse and neglect in particular families, rather than promoting the welfare of children who are regarded as being at risk. What preventive services there are have tended to be provided by the voluntary sector and to have a history of poor funding. In emphasizing the need for the introduction of a range of child care services, Ferguson (1995) draws on his own research into the numbers of cases of reported child abuse which are filtered out at each stage of investigation. A further aspect of the problem of the lack of an integrated child care system in Ireland is the significant divergences in child protection practice from region to region, and even between different community care areas within regions – for example, Kenny (1995) highlights the differences in the use of court orders. The lack of resources available for social workers to provide anything other than crisis services, and their increasing workload in dealing with child abuse cases, are recurring themes in the literature. Richardson (1994), in a paper presented to the Irish Association of Social Workers, drew attention to the fact that, while the government refers to the development of family services, it gives no indication as to what form these should take. This concern with the provision of a range of child care services holds particular resonance for services in rural Ireland, according to Donnelly (1994). He argues that in small communities, highly professional and visible child protection services are not appropriate, particularly where there are strong community networks with an ambivalence to interference by professionals and the state. He believes that there is a unique opportunity in rural communities to bring about lasting change in attitudes to child protection if services are delivered in the context of child welfare, such as public health, education, social recreation and the linking of every family to these services, as opposed to a focus on the child protection context. Donnelly advocates the introduction of multi-disciplinary child welfare teams, based locally and involving local community leaders.

Mandatory reporting

Ferguson (1995) refers to figures for sources of referral in child abuse cases in Ireland which illustrate the increasing percentage of referrals that are coming from professionals. He notes that this indicates a profound historical transformation in reporting patterns in child abuse cases – as up to the 1950s only 20 per cent of cases reported to the Irish Society for the Prevention of Cruelty to Children came from professional sources. However, in comparison to the USA, where mandatory reporting has been in operation since the 1960s, Irish professionals are still under-reporting. Anna Kelly, a public health nurse, states that in Ireland, the consequences of intervening too precipitously weigh heavily on the minds of professionals. Many are still very uncomfortable with having to deal with 'at risk' situations, especially when the individuals involved are known to them – as is often the case with public health nurses (Kelly, 1995). Clearly this problem will be particularly pertinent in Ireland's many small, close-knit, rural communities.

The Kilkenny Incest Report recommended the introduction of mandatory reporting and in April 1995 the government took the first steps towards the implementation of this recommendation by publishing procedures for co-operation between social workers and the *gardai*. The procedures oblige social workers and *gardai* to notify each other if they suspect a child has been physically or sexually abused and to agree on a joint strategy for investigation. The guidelines were afforded a cautious welcome, with a number of concerns being raised about how they will work in practice. The Irish Association of Social Workers welcomed the guidelines but is concerned at the need for social workers to inform the *gardai* **immediately** abuse is suspected. They fear that this could lead to an increase in the number of unfounded allegations and the consequent impact on families from the investigative process itself which could interfere with their attempts to establish relationships with the parents involved and affect their ability to provide support to the family, particularly their aim of helping parents to develop parenting skills (O'Morain, 1995). There is also fear that immediate reporting of suspicions to the *gardai* will put parents under further stress and could, in fact, result in other members of the family not reporting any suspicions they may have about abuse because of the need to involve the *gardai* immediately. An editorial in the *Irish Times* (1995), commenting on the guidelines, refers to the guilt which children involved in suspected abuse cases may feel for bringing 'trouble', in the form of the police, onto their family. The argument is that social workers must have some scope to work with families before contacting the *gardai* (the procedures do, in fact, allow scope to a certain extent by permitting social workers to consult with other professionals before establishing whether grounds for suspected abuse do exist).

A consultative process on mandatory reporting was initiated by the minister of state at the Departments of Health, Education and Justice with special responsibility for children, with the launch, in February 1996, of *Putting Children First – Discussion Document on Mandatory Reporting*. Over two hundred submissions from groups and individuals were received and the consultative process culminated in a consultative forum held in September 1996 at which the majority of participants expressed reservations or opposition to mandatory reporting (Department of Health, 1997b). The idea of improved co-operation and co-ordination between professionals and agencies as a means of addressing the problems that currently exist in relation to the reporting of child abuse received much attention and support. In general, it seems that the guidelines for co-operation between social workers and *gardai* provided a good framework and that initiatives to strengthen existing arrangements for reporting of child abuse would be in the best interests of children together with advances in joint training (Buckley, 1995). Monitoring and evaluation over a three-year period was favoured as the way forward. In the light of concern about the suitability of those working with children, the Department of Health agreed with the *gardai* a system for screening which will ensure that child care staff will undergo *garda* checks concerning their suitability to work with children. In their 1994–1995 Annual Report, the Irish Association of Social Workers called for a similar directive to apply to social workers and to other professionals who come into close contact with children (Kirwan, 1995).

Increasing workloads of social workers

Social workers are increasingly drawing attention to the immense struggles and difficulties they face working in the child care and child protection areas because of inadequate resources. Some social work teams are experiencing a crisis due to unmanageable workload levels. For example, during 1995, social workers in Dublin's north inner city refused to take on new cases, claiming that there were already 100 cases known to them but receiving no services. Social workers are increasingly involved in crisis work only, but even here they spend most of their time on the telephone trying to arrange scarce placements for children or supervising access visits, rather than concentrating on the therapeutic/counselling aspects of social work with families and children in crisis.

The development of a child-centred approach

The Irish Constitution is extremely unusual in the importance it places on the rights of the family and parents and in the authority it invests in them (in the constitution 'the family' was defined as 'the married family' only, up to the referendum result of 15 November 1995). This emphasis on the privacy of the family has created an ambivalence towards child protection generally: on the one hand there is outrage at the apparent failure of social workers to take action to protect children, yet on the other there is public concern at a perceived over-interference by the state in family life. For example, an organization of parents was formed in opposition to the Stay Safe Programme introduced in primary schools. The group argues that child sexual abuse is not as prevalent as the programme suggests and that the programme will lead to break-up of the family. (It should be noted that there has been debate about the Stay Safe Programme amongst professionals as well. Gogarty (1995) argues, for example, that as the child becomes attached to those who care for her/him it becomes difficult for the child to judge good and bad feelings. This may lead to the child blaming her/himself for not making the right assessments of such feelings.)

It is within this context of a historic and constitutional emphasis on the rights of the family, the authority of parents and a lack of reference to the rights of children, that social workers are attempting to develop a child-centred approach to child care work. Looking at one example of ongoing work in the area of developing a child-centred approach, Gogarty (1995) describes the work of the Donegal Treatment Team set up in 1989 in order to deal with children in care who were presenting with major disruptions and fostering breakdowns. She refers to two essential elements in enhancing the well-being of children in care: first, a sense of continuity in belonging to a family to which the child feels him/herself fully attached (i.e. the foster parents or residential child care workers); and second, a sense of identity which is best achieved by continued contact with important people in the past (i.e. own birth family – parents, siblings, extended family). Gogarty identifies two problems in current service provision. These are: that prevention services are too broadly based and do not direct themselves clearly enough at specific families where care proceedings are a possibility; and that intervention tools are not subtle enough to analyse and repair problems in the attachment process between children and parents. Interventions should be made at an earlier stage.

The Travelling community

While the last section dealt with issues concerning the development of a child-centred approach by social workers, one important element is the development of a child-centred approach which is flexible enough to respond to cultural diversity. Kilmurray and Richardson (1994, p.126) note how there is a lack of recognition in Ireland of the existence of differing cultures and that, in fact, 'considerable pride is often expressed in the relative homogeneity of Irish society. In policy terms this can be translated into a denial of the existence of individual or institutional racism.' One of the groups most affected in Ireland is the Travelling community, of whom there are approximately 20,000 in Ireland. For example: Travellers have more than double the national rate of stillbirths; the infant mortality rate for Travellers is three times the national average; their life expectancy is the same as that which settled people expected in the 1940s; and the education system ignores the fact that Travellers have a distinct dialect of their own. Moloney notes that the majority of community care social workers who deal with child and child protection issues at some time work with Traveller families. However, she points out that the 1991 Child Care Act makes no mention of any cultural, ethnic or racial considerations in relation to taking children into care. This means in effect that 'there is no legal obligation on the health board therefore to attempt to provide culturally appropriate placements for Traveller children in need of care' (Moloney, 1994, p.42). The Irish Association of Social Workers inaugurated a Special Interest Group on Travellers in February 1994. They are particularly interested in developments which aim for Traveller families to become foster parents for Traveller children and to utilize the extended family tradition to provide support for Traveller families in times of crisis (Guthrie, 1995).

Youth homelessness

Section 5 of the 1991 Child Care Act places a statutory responsibility on health boards to provide reasonable, suitable and appropriate accommodation for homeless children. In late 1992/93 a controversy erupted over the placement of healthy children in hospital due to a lack of alternative care. This practice continues and remains an issue of ongoing tension. Analysing the implementation of section 5 of the 1991 Child Care Act (which was one of the first statutory sections of the Act to be implemented by health boards), O'Sullivan (1995) found that health boards have insufficient facilities for homeless children and are increasingly relying on bed and breakfast accommodation. This gives rise to a concern regarding the commitment of the state to promote the welfare of homeless children. Focus Point, a key voluntary organization that works with up to 4,000 homeless young people and adults per year, was one of the many organizations calling on the government to implement fully the Child Care Act and to provide urgently needed facilities which must be planned to meet a range of accommodation needs for children and young people: emergency needs, short-term needs and long-term needs.

Domestic violence

Hegarty (1993), writing as vice-chair of Women's Aid, argues that many women who are experiencing violence and abuse in their homes are afraid to make contact with social workers for a variety of reasons, and that any contact they do have with social workers is usually in relation to the welfare of their children. She states that this gives women the message that their lives are of secondary importance and that it is essential that social workers do not focus solely on the child protection issues at the expense of investigating and aiding women who are experiencing domestic violence. In winter 1993 the Irish Association of Social Workers, recognizing the importance of this area, called on the Minister for Health to initiate research into family violence.

Residential child care: Social workers and child care workers

There are under 1,000 children in residential care in Ireland, accommodated in group homes, special schools, adolescent units and psychiatric units. If it was the Kilkenny Incest Report which first drew attention to the extent of child abuse within the family context in Ireland, then it was the inquiry into child sexual abuse at Madonna House, a residential child care facility, which focused attention on the activities of the residential sector (Ireland 1996b). Children in care are dependent on three sets of primary relationships: with parents, social workers and child care workers. The division historically between social workers and child care workers may mean that social workers do not get close enough to children in care and to their care workers. McLellan (1994) observes 'an irrational sense of apathy and ambivalence towards residential childcare' (p.10). He suggests that some social workers view residential child care practices as outmoded; the fact that social work training is university-based and child care training is not raises issues of status differences. More investigation is required into the relationship of social workers to residential care.

Social work with other client groups

There are 'some' social workers working with older people. A major area of work for them is the implementation of the 1990 Health (Nursing Homes) Act, particularly with the entitlement of some older people to free or subsidized nursing home care. The legislation concerning the payment of fees to nursing homes is complex and its operation is time-consuming. In the 1994–1995 Annual Report of the Irish Association of Social Workers, the Specialist Interest Group on Ageing reported that the group would be concentrating in the coming year on lobbying for changes in the implementation of aspects of the Act. The group had spent the year concentrating on providing a support forum for social workers working with older people, and promoting the concept of social work with older people as being a worthwhile and challenging area in which to work. Other plans for the future included working towards expanding community care teams to include social workers with older people, getting elder abuse recognized as an issue, and highlighting ongoing deficiencies in services in the community (Cagney, 1995; O'Loughlin, 1995).

Organization: The employment base of social work

The appointment of social workers in any great numbers can be traced to 1971. The implementation of the 1970 Health Act, with the consequent reform of the administrative arrangements for the delivery of health and personal social services, built on initiatives in the 1960s and reflected a broad concern with a range of population groups and involvement of social workers in the development of community social services. The personal social services in Ireland are provided by a mixed economy of welfare involving a range of partners. Better co-ordination and co-operation in the planning and delivery of services is a recurring theme.

Social work education and training

Ireland, 'perhaps surprisingly', notes Lorenz (1994, p.44), has a completely secular, university-based approach to social work education. The churches promoted the inception of social work training in the 1930s in the then largely Protestant Trinity College Dublin and the then largely Catholic University College Dublin. Social work education is confined to the universities and up to the 1980s, Irish social work courses provided in University College Dublin, University College Cork and Trinity College Dublin were validated by the United Kingdom Central Council for Education and Training in Social Work (CCETSW). Irish social workers were awarded the Certificate of Qualification in Social Work (CQSW).

Following a decision by CCETSW in the 1980s to cease its involvement in Irish social work education, an *ad hoc* committee on social work was set up by the minister for health to advise on the 'qualifications necessary for appointment as a social worker under a health board' (Department of Health, 1993,

Introduction). At the Annual Conference of the Irish Association of Social Workers in 1994, the Minister indicated his intention to launch a validation body in order to 'maintain the recommended standards of social work education and training in Ireland' (Department of Health, 1993, para. 1.1). The National Validation Body on Social Work Qualifications was established in 1995. The board was re-named the National Social Work Qualifications Board (NSWQB) and established by statutory instrument (SI No 97 of 1997), by the minister for health in April 1997. The board has a wide range of functions which include: granting the National Qualification in Social Work (NQSW) to persons who have successfully completed recognized courses of study; advising on the equivalence of qualifications obtained outside Ireland; advising the minister, health boards and other agencies as to which courses have been recognized by the NSWQB; advising the minister on standards which should inform education and training of social workers in the state; assessing on a regular basis the suitability of the social work education and training provided by the institutions recognized by the board.

Themes and issues

Role and status of the personal social services in Ireland

The personal social services in Ireland have traditionally received less attention than other social policy areas in terms of legislation, funding, administrative back-up, training and research. In November 1991, the Mid Western Health Board (one of eight health boards responsible for the administration of health and personal social services) held a conference on the personal social services. The theme was 'Partnership in Practice: The Future of the Personal Social Services'. Contributors from various voluntary, statutory, community and academic backgrounds discussed ways to enhance partnership between the health boards, other statutory services and professionals, voluntary agencies, clients and informal networks, not only through co-ordination in the planning and delivery of services, but also through developing a holistic approach to need, taking account of financial, emotional, psychological and social needs, both at government policy level and at the level of local provision (Mid Western Health Board, 1991). The emphasis on partnership follows on from, and reinforces, a long tradition of voluntarism and self-help in the provision of personal social services and social care. The importance of the role of the voluntary and community sectors is recognized in all areas of social service provision in Ireland. In November 1996, the minister for health in announcing plans for restructuring the largest health board in the country confirmed that 'all services, both voluntary and statutory, will be funded by the new Authority, facilitating more integrated planning, delivery and evaluation of health and personal social services in the area' (Department of Health, 1996b). A long-awaited policy document on the voluntary and community sector under the title *Supporting the Voluntary Sector* finally provides a framework to examine issues in relation to funding of voluntary organizations, participation in policy-making, structures for voluntary activity at national and regional level and presents guidelines for the statutory and voluntary sectors in terms of good practice (Ireland, 1997).

Social work as an element of the personal social services

Given the fact that the personal social services have traditionally been treated as the 'poor relation' in the field of social policy, then it is not surprising to find that social work itself has been treated in much the same way. It was not until the passing of the 1970 Health Act and the creation of community care programmes in each health board that social workers in Ireland were employed in any great numbers. The community care programme provided for the delivery of locally-based multi-disciplinary services by teams of doctors, dentists, social workers, health inspectors and home assistance (community welfare) officers. The introduction of social workers as the newest professionals in the community care programme as it was devised in the early 1970s was not without problems in the ensuing years. Since then a dual thrust of primary healthcare and personal social services has emerged in an uneasy alliance under a vague rubric and in an *ad hoc* fashion rather than any systematic planned development. Ambivalence about the appropriate mix of statutory and voluntary services in meeting health and welfare needs is reflected in an absence of clear policy goals for the development of social work services within the entire statutory sector, and a confused picture around the extent and nature of the voluntary sector (Lavan, 1991).

Legislation in relation to social work in Ireland

The 1970 Health Act can be identified as a major milestone in the development of social work in Ireland. In the words of one commentator, the 1991 Child Care Act is 'probably the most significant development in the history of social work services (in Ireland) since the 1970 Health Act' (Clarke, 1991, p.13). By the end of 1996, all sections of the 1991 Act had been implemented. The 1996 Child Care Plan sets out new child care developments approved for each health board; provisions include:

- an increase in the fostering allowance for children over 12 years;
- the provision of additional emergency, special foster care places;
- the provision of additional accommodation and supports for out-of-home young people;

- improvements in treatment services for victims of child abuse;
- increased funding for preventative services such as family resources centres, youth projects and day nurseries.

Under the 1991 Child Care Act each health board must publish an *annual review of child care and family support services* and submit this to the minister for health. Such a review provides the basis, finally, for the development of a coherent picture of practice on the ground. The Irish Association of Social Workers (IASW, 1997), meeting with the minister of state, prior to the annual social work conference, highlighted their concerns around the following issues:

- the need for a quality development of a Guardian ad Litem service;
- the need to progress the establishment of the Social Services Inspectorate;
- continuing concern about the placement of healthy (homeless) children in hospital beds because of a shortage of emergency accommodation;
- the need for progress on the creation of a post of Ombudsman for Children.

A new 1996 Children Bill concerned primarily with young offenders is making its way through the Irish parliament in 1997. Speaking at a conference in Dublin early in 1997, on the 1996 Children Bill, Professor Norman Tutt predicted that the state's eight health boards will come under 'tremendous pressure' as a result of the impact of this additional legislation which will mean that by the end of the 1990s, the largest health authority in the country will have all its social work resources 'soaked up' in meeting child protection needs (*Irish Times*, 1997). One element of the new bill which has attracted approval from some social work commentators is the proposal for the development of a 'Diversion Programme' which relies heavily on the involvement of the family of the young person and in particular advocates the use of the 'Family Conference' model. The involvement of children and young persons in the plans which are to affect them is a sound principle. However, attendance by children or young persons at such case/family conferences does not necessarily guarantee their participation. While in Ireland *attendance* is being heralded as good practice, this is another example of the need for research to answer a range of questions, for example whether children and young persons do participate, and if so, how do they actually participate?

A commitment to establish a Social Services Inspectorate (Department of Health, 1997b), intended to facilitate improved service provision and child care practice, could provide the leadership needed to bring together all the elements required for a sound and integrated child care service. In relation to the development of a child-centred approach in Ireland a number of commentators advocate that serious consideration should be given to the introduction of an ombudsman for children and a commitment has been given in principle to this development (Department of Health, 1997b).

Endword

If and when the 1996 Children Bill becomes law, this piece of legislation together with the 1991 Child Care Act will finally update the 1908 Children Act which was the central piece of legislation in relation to children throughout this century. It is salutary to acknowledge that it will have taken ninety years to update the law in relation to children in Ireland. The passing of legislation, the formulation of policy, the development of administrative structures are slow and ponderous. One can only hope that the twenty-first century will witness a revolution in policy-making and implementation which will better serve the needs of children.

In this chapter it has only been possible to focus on *some* of the contemporary issues related to social work in Ireland. Further research is required in order to build up a picture of the way social work is developing, across a range of employment sectors. The time has come to assess how social workers fit into the larger social policy agenda in Ireland and the way in which they contribute to the development of social work policy. The implications of the involvement of Irish social workers in European and international networks suggest another avenue of exploration.

This chapter has discussed the role of social workers in child care and child protection work. There are two major concerns about social work in Ireland. First, other client groups experience limited social work input because of the profession's identification with the field of child care. Second, within the context of social work and child care, an almost total concentration on crisis involvement and child protection work means that family support services, preventive work and community social work are severely under-resourced.

Reference has been made to the shortage of child care research in Ireland and problems in the dissemination of findings. The fear is that policy and practice may be developed in a piecemeal fashion without either reference to empirical research findings or theoretical frameworks of analysis. Wider questions arise about the shaping of Irish social policy and the impact of global transformation on national policies. In particular it is necessary to continually re-examine the connections between poverty, especially child poverty, child care, child protection, juvenile justice, structural inequalities, gender discrimination, and issues of class, status and power.

5 Social work in Italy

Anna Maria Cavallone and Franca Ferrario

Translated by Ernesta Rogers

Introduction: Social work and policies in health and social services in the last few decades

In Italy, social work is defined by the term *servizio sociale*, which means the professional activities of qualified social workers – workers holding a legally-recognized diploma. This diploma is obtained after a three-year course which includes both theory and practice in its curriculum. At present, such courses are part of university studies, leading to the diploma, a first-level university qualification (*diploma universitario di primo grado*). As a profession in its present form, social work in Italy developed immediately after the end of the Second World War, with the return of democracy and in a climate of reconstruction. Social work has continuously developed the practice, training and basic theoretical knowledge, but there has been a fundamental continuity in the profession's values, objectives and methods.

In order to understand present trends, it is helpful to review the more significant events of the past few decades.

Recent developments: The 1970s and 1980s

As early as the 1960s, both the basic philosophy and the organization of health and social services were subject to considerable criticism. The main reasons for the criticisms were: the large number of agencies providing services; the fact that most of them were very centralized in their management and very distant from the users, and a heavy reliance on institutions both in the health field and in social welfare agencies (not least because many institutions were receiving residents who had come a long way from their natural environment, and were run by unqualified staff). During this period, significant developments have been the 'anti-psychiatric movement' and the movements against marginalization, the feminist movement and others, supported by various political, Catholic and trade union groups, which have influenced social policy and social work practice.

During the 1970s, several laws of reform were approved by parliament, of which the most significant were, firstly, legislation concerning the devolution of powers regarding health and social services, through which regional authorities were made responsible for legislating, planning and administering the funds allocated to them by the central government, while central government retained the central functions of providing guidelines and co-ordinating activities of regional authorities. At the same time, the organization and management of services were devolved to the municipalities (*comuni*) – in the case of large conurbations to sub-divisions of the municipalities (*circoscrizioni*), in the case of small municipalities to groups of them comprising larger areas (*consorzi*). These changes were made possible by the suppression of most of the large national welfare agencies which existed before (Law no.616/1977).

Secondly, a law was passed establishing a national health service (Law no.833/1978), giving the right to all citizens to receive healthcare, and replacing the old system whereby different categories of workers received different standards of care according to their insurance contributions. This new law also established the local health units (*unità sanitarie locali* – USL – and their subdivisions – districts), responsible for the implementation of the health service.

As a result of the political and cultural debate of the time, the legislation embodies some fundamental principles, such as:

- a global approach to problems and the integration of health and social services;
- an emphasis on preventive action;
- devolution of services management, with a stress on the participation of local communities;
- de-institutionalization, and the provision of services and care in the community.

The activities of the health units are intended to be integrated and co-ordinated with the social services, which are the responsibility of the local authority (primary social services, financial assistance, advice and information centres on welfare rights, home help, daycare and residential care).

Social workers are employed mostly within the social services run by the local authority and in the health services of the USL: their role does not merely consist of providing services to individual users, but also involves assessing collective needs in the area of their jurisdiction (*territorio*), contributing thereby to the planning of services, and networking with existing institutions, voluntary groups, etc., to seek better solutions to community problems.

This close contact with the community, in all its aspects, gives social workers knowledge of the roots of local dysfunctions and difficulties, cultural components of problems, and potential local resources. Also, such knowledge feeds into their way of working with direct users, and simultaneously allows them to operate preventively, so that there is constant innovation in the services that are offered to the local population.

The implementation of the reforms shows a great diversity in the various regions of the country. Different organizational models have been followed, so that in some cases the integration between health and social services has been a success, while in other areas social services are run in part or totally by the local authorities, and co-ordination with the local health units is achieved through various forms of agreement. There is still a lack of national legislation concerning general guidelines for social services and social welfare, including financial assistance. Some regional authorities have legislated in this field, and organized accordingly. The changes and development of diversified services according to these new principles have led to the development of new social professions, such as domiciliary helpers or care assistants, while new variations in the roles of more established professionals have emerged, as in the case of *educatori* (equivalent to the French *educateurs*) and psychologists.

Furthermore, sociologists have increasingly been employed within the social services field with research and management functions. All this has stimulated studies and research aimed at defining specific traits and common aspects of the various professions, as well as the possibilities of constructive co-operation.

During this time, the schools of social work (both private and public) faced a situation of great uncertainty, as the diploma they conferred had no legal value or recognition. There were two different possibilities: either social work schools could become part of the universities (which many felt the appropriate setting for a good scientific level of training and for proper social recognition of social workers' status in comparison with other professions) or social work training might have become part of vocational training, for which the regional education authorities have responsibility, and would then be more closely targeted at local services needs.

This pressure for official legitimization of the profession through a more academic education stimulated the production of several theoretical studies on social work, bringing to the fore issues concerning methodology that had been neglected in the preceding years when the political component of the professional role had been particularly stressed. After a long struggle by all the professional organizations (such as the National Association of Social Workers and the Association of Social Work Teachers) in the 1980s, they gained recognition that the diploma conferred by the schools of social work, which formed part of some universities as schools under a special statute, was equivalent to a university diploma, and that education provided by the schools constituted basic training for the social work profession. However, social workers are still employed in state and local authority services at a level which is totally inconsistent with their training and their responsibilities, due to the fact that in the civil service and in the career structure of local authorities, a degree is needed (university qualification at the second level) in order to work in middle and higher management.

During the 1980s, debates around the whole concept of the welfare state, the possibilities of its practical implementation, and the reforms needed – debates which still continue – stimulated a process of redistribution of responsibilities among state, voluntary and private organizations and the market, aiming at a more effective mix of welfare services by different providers.

Current context: The 1990s

In the second half of the 1990s, social workers have to operate in a very difficult political and economic context. It seems very unlikely that social services and health services are to be given high priority. Italy has a high national debt, there have been considerable cuts in public spending, and unemployment is very high, even though there are signs of some economic recovery. The number of people with inadequate incomes is increasing. The Italian commission for the study of poverty and social exclusion, a commission established by the Presidency of the Council of Ministers, reports that in 1995 there were 6,696,000 people living on less than half the average income, with a higher percentage in the south (Commissione di indagine sulla povertà e sull'emarginazione, 1995). Furthermore, there is a large group of very poor people (people with no fixed abode, people suffering from mental disturbance, illegal immigrants at the margin of society and Travellers). The problems of this group are at the same time problems of economic poverty, and problems of social exclusion and failure of personal relationships.

The problems connected with poverty and social exclusion are a challenge to economic and social policies, to personal social services both private and statutory, and to society as a whole. The results of such problems weigh heavily on social workers' activities: they have to spend a lot of energy in finding – and not always succeeding in finding – resources to satisfy basic, primary needs, while there is little opportunity for work aimed at fostering initiatives and promoting activities that would help individual development and social cohesion.

Social workers can easily appear to act as a buffer in emergency situations, but always operating at the margins of the real problem, reacting rather than dealing with the basic issues. However, as is shown in the next section, there are situations, even now, in which social workers are operating within effective and well-thought-out projects.

The debate around social policies and the welfare state continues. A renewed emphasis is being placed on the educational and caring functions of the family as well as on the importance of public policies, and measures and services supporting these functions. A new emphasis is also being placed on community solidarity. The general orientation of central government is to take responsibility for the provision of state guidelines and co-ordination functions, while the actual provision of services is increasingly carried out through voluntary and non-profitmaking organizations, generally through *ad hoc* agreements.

Two significant pieces of legislation have been passed recently concerning the use of volunteers and social co-operatives.

The law on organizations making use of volunteers (Law no.266/1991) gives recognition to the importance of voluntary work, and sets down the legal requirements for the agreements that can be made between statutory agencies and these organizations. This law has given new impetus to the debate about the role and responsibilities of statutory and private, non-profitmaking agencies, and about the conditions for effective collaboration between them.

Social co-operatives are regulated by Law no.381/1991, and they include co-operative associations that manage and provide services in the fields of health, social welfare and education or work co-operatives, aiming at the economic production of goods and services, in various fields, with the purpose of ensuring work for people with various kinds of disabilities. In work co-operatives, disabled people must constitute at least 30 per cent of the co-operative membership. These organizations are valuable instruments to promote a policy of social integration, as long as the state maintains a role of guarantor of the quality of the services offered, as well as of their low cost. This role must be active not just at the time of signing the agreement, but also in the assessment of results.

Finally, we can mention recent regulation of the social work profession: this includes legislation concerning the establishment of the profession, and instituting a register and a professional order (Law no.84/1993, and its general regulations, Law no.615/1994) and the establishment of a university first-level diploma of social work (Ministry of Education Decree, 23/5/1994), fully integrated in the university structure, which consolidates the position of social work training compared with the previous diploma offered by the schools with a special statute.

Legislation is pending for the establishment of a full degree course in social work; this will constitute fuller recognition for the profession, as it will open the way to higher managerial responsibilities and to doctoral studies, also a necessary qualification for social work teaching posts. The professional organizations are campaigning actively for this, and in the 1990s there is added pressure from a recently-established trade union of social workers (SUNAS).

Practice: Recent developments in social work practice

Some general considerations

Even though there is a high degree of diversity within the institutional settings and organizational systems in which social workers operate, it is possible to identify some significant innovations developing in social work practice. The changes concern:

- types of users;
- roles undertaken by social workers, and their methods of working;
- various forms of co-operation with other professions and within communities.

Several interacting factors have contributed to this evolution in practice, for example:

- increased reflection on professional identity, and interesting experimentation (in some local authorities and USLs);
- the general trend in national legislation towards avoiding institutionalization and helping users remain in their normal environment;
- greater dissemination of research findings in the social sciences;
- the need to address and prevent new and increasingly complex material, social and relational needs through more differentiated responses from statutory and private agencies;
- a simultaneous process of renewal in other social and health professions also seeking their own identity and to redefine their operational boundaries;
- the increasing presence of private, non-profitmaking organizations.

These developments have all emphasized the importance of a multi-functional approach in social work, and in particular the typical social work role of connecting needs and resources in the helping process to individuals (especially to the more disadvantaged users). This activity of connection, as part of a global plan to provide help, is now considered central. There is a stress on making the best use of what is available through good organization, through the promotion of new initiatives, and the participation of local communities and local groups, given that at present the gap between needs and resources is becoming increasingly apparent. There is also recognition of the need to sharpen innovative techniques and methodologies in social work, both in casework and in community work, such as inter-agency co-ordination, project work, networking, mediation work, assessment, support to participative practice and new forms of inter-professional co-operation.

Current social work practice: Children and families

In the area of child and family welfare, social workers have been committed for the last two decades both to the development of alternatives to placement in children's homes and to new programmes for the promotion of a healthy family life and child development. This professional orientation resulted from a wide-ranging debate which introduced new legislation that recognized and reinforced the rights of children, and also important laws regarding women's rights and reforms in family law.

Institutionalization was the most common form of intervention until legislation was passed concerning fostering and adoption (Law no.184/1983). Even today, the objective of de-institutionalization has not been attained, as there are still around 40,000 children in children's homes. Recently, alongside increases in adoption and fostering, there have been developments in other forms of intervention, which aim to keep the children in their home environment: for example, day fostering; educational assistance within the family or in the neighbourhood; initiatives for parental education, and projects for educational, recreational and vocational activities in the community. An interesting development has been the type of intervention promoted by both some local authorities (for instance, the family centres established by the Emilia Romagne region) and private agencies to mobilize families in a given geographical area, to create opportunities for mutual help, so families themselves become resources, participating in the analysis of the particular needs of the area and also in planning more adequate responses to support children and families.

Greater co-operation is developing between different institutions and professions, and between statutory agencies and voluntary organizations offering educational services both for residential and daycare. Social workers, at least in some areas, have been able to use new approaches to problems associated with children and families as ecological system theories have become better known and skills in networking have become more sophisticated.

There has also been a development in the relationship between social workers and the professional *educatori* (pedagogical workers) who, in some regions, operate alongside in rehabilitative and preventive activities. For example, domiciliary educational help, or neighbourhood educational help, is an example of this type of co-operation. This service has been available for several years in cities like Milan and Turin, and is targeted particularly at children who live in 'at risk' areas who are already showing difficulties in their adjustment to school or in social relationships. These *educatori* often belong to co-operatives that have a contract with the local authority. Social workers and educators also co-operate in projects concerning all the children living in a given area, in street work and in planning promotional or preventive action, also in co-operation with schools.

This type of assistance consists of offering a personal relationship with specialized *educatori* to children in need. A care plan is agreed, aiming to provide opportunities for emotional growth and for the development of positive relationships within the family, the school, work and the social environment. Attention is also given to generating opportunities for encounters and meeting with other children and families in the area. Care plans for the children are part of larger projects (co-ordinated by the area social worker) which also involve providing help to families in order to support their capacity to cope so that they can resume their proper educational role and their relationship with the school.

Because of the great social changes now happening in Italy, social workers have had to deal with new needs, and problems among different client groups. One example might be helping children of immigrants or Travellers to settle in school. Such action is often part of a larger project aimed at counteracting social exclusion, and at helping these groups to find their place in the community. Action is also being taken to help the children of HIV-positive mothers.

A developing area of intervention is family mediation – help for families already separated, or in the process of separation, so that family relationships can be re-organized, and appropriate roles maintained. There is now specific training for professionals involved in family mediation, which is open to psychologists and social workers alike.

In recent times, an issue which has attracted particular attention and has been the object of research is the problem of child abuse. It has always been difficult in cases of child abuse to fulfil the double role of control and help. However, there have been positive experiences, in which a court order gives social workers a degree of social control and makes it possible to plan for the protection and care of the child, while providing opportunities for family rehabilitation. A core issue is the need for court and social workers to share the same fundamental principles of intervention, and for their respective roles to be well-defined and clearly presented from the beginning.

A critical area of social work concerns multi-problem families, where unsatisfied primary needs interact with conflict and family break-up as well as social exclusion. Alongside emergency intervention, such cases require long-term intervention and co-operation between different professionals to enable a proper assessment of the problems and choice of an appropriate care plan. Intervention in such situations presents two sets of difficulties: on one hand a real lack of financial resources, adequate housing, employment and alternative viable solutions outside the family; on the other, difficulties due to the heavy workloads of social workers, who often operate without appropriate supportive supervision or professional consultation, and experience lack of co-operation in implementing the care plans – psychiatrists and psychologists often seem to stop at the stage of assessment and diagnosis. These professionals are often more oriented to strictly clinical work and private practice, and are not always available for team work dealing with poorly-motivated clients in social and family situations of great complexity.

More recently, attention has been given to the problem of battered women. Special telephone helplines have been activated, and in some cities emergency services and shelters for women and children have been made available.

Older people

The ageing of the population (this is a very significant pattern in a country with a very low birth rate of 1.3 and a life expectancy among the highest), and the increasing number of dependent old people in need of constant health and personal care, have brought changes to the practice area, also following the new approaches to combat social exclusion, and a global approach to health and social care. Social work has found a new occupational space in relation to integrated domiciliary help, dealing with both health and social needs; domiciliary hospital care; daycare fostering for isolated old people; new forms of residential healthcare; group living; day centres; self-help groups, and various other forms of voluntary help.

The Target Project for the protection of older people's health is part of current national health plans and has supported these approaches. It includes the provision of a multi-professional first-contact team called the Geriatric Assessment Team, including health professionals and social workers. The task of the team is to assess individual situations, prepare an individualized care plan, and to give appropriate responses in an integrated form.

This new approach to the welfare of older people, together with the large number of statutory and private organizations involved, has placed considerable demands on the organization of co-operation between different professionals and institutions. Different solutions have been chosen by different local authorities, and some options are still being considered and studied. Social workers, along with casework activities, are also involved in the planning, organization and assessment of the services with the other professionals. In particular, social workers have a crucial role in co-operating with home help services, to ensure that domiciliary help becomes an integral part of care plans.

Older people have a variety of needs, requiring a 'package' of provisions from public or private services, and support from volunteers. The effectiveness of this type of service delivery depends very much on the presence of a social worker capable of making an organic plan who is also able to stimulate co-operation between the various helpers and the user's network of relationships. Co-operation between hospitals and social services is very important, particularly at the time of formulating a discharge plan for older people with complex health and social needs.

While there is an increase in the number of fragile old people (even in those social classes that traditionally would not make use of public services), social workers have also centred their attention on active older people, trying to support them in their ordinary social life, to encourage interaction with the younger generation, and help in the formation of self-help groups. Many active older people take part in socially useful activities as volunteers, and participate in movements to defend their own rights, so they also become a resource for the community.

Attention is also given to the needs of carers, who are often quite old themselves, and often at risk because of the stress and the physical work involved in caring for even older relatives over long periods of time. In response to these needs, individual and group counselling services are expanding, as well as respite services and support from self-help groups.

Social work and justice

The Ministry of Justice in Italy employs about 1,600 social workers. New developments are taking place in the provision of social services for people subject to penal measures. In the last few years, ministry social workers have established a group called Co-ordination of the Justice Social Workers. This group has initiated a process of reflection and study on the role of the ministry's social services, particularly where prevention of deviance is concerned, and the rehabilitation of offenders – all within a policy framework designed to minimize custodial sentences.

Prison overcrowding is a serious problem, and this and the need for rehabilitative penal measures has brought into focus the need for alternatives. Such measures are envisioned in legislation, but not very extensively used by the courts (e.g. supervision by social workers, probation, etc.). The adults' sector of the ministry of social services is already working through projects, established in co-operation with local authorities, social co-operatives and associations, which aim to rehabilitate offenders on licence or parole through alternative measures. These projects can re-introduce prisoners into social life through work or community activities.

Mental health

In the field of mental health, Law no.180/1978, which initiated reforms in the care of psychiatric patients, envisaged the closure of mental hospitals and the establishment of wards for the diagnosis and treatment of patients in the acute phase of mental illness in special wings of general hospitals. This law also established day hospitals, day centres and a large variety of residential services (e.g. therapeutic communities, family groups, residential communities, psychosocial help services). Implementation of the law has been slow, particularly in some parts of the country, but health and social workers in this field are increasingly engaged in a struggle against social exclusion, and to protect the civil, social and economic rights of mentally ill patients.

The focus for the social worker is not only to assess correctly and use, as far as possible, the inner resources of the person, but also to create the most favourable conditions in his/her environment to promote positive social interaction. A particularly important consideration in the care plan is ensuring that help is given to cope with everyday life and enable the person to improve their level of autonomy and independence. Key instruments to achieve this are: financial support to which patients may be entitled (and most need to use); sheltered accommodation or protected lodgings; day centres supporting recreational activities, and a return to work through social co-operatives. Consideration is also given by social workers to supporting patients' families, and wherever possible, involving family members in rehabilitation.

Social workers are also involved in helping in the promotion of associations between users, volunteers and social practitioners, and they support initiatives for setting up informal groups.

A stimulating current debate is in progress, centring on the role of primary social services in relation to the specialized psychiatric services. There is a general tendency to encourage primary services to deal as far as possible with mentally ill users without excluding and relegating them to special enclaves, and so hiding the social malaise of mental illness. Another issue of current debate concerns the role of social workers in psychiatric services, particularly how specialized social work should be in this field. There is an obvious need for social workers to have a deeper knowledge about mental illness than is normally provided in basic training. Also, the methods used by social workers must relate to the characteristics of the users, but there is also a need not to alter the characteristics of the profession by excessive 'psychiatrization'.

Social work and immigration

The growing presence of foreign immigrants in Italy, whether legal or illegal, has been a matter of concern, particularly for some local authorities which have opened special social services sections to work with immigrants (e.g. in Bergamo and Udine). Various projects for work with immigrants have been developed in different parts of the country, and four main approaches can be distinguished:

- establishing co-ordination between statutory and voluntary organizations offering assistance to immigrants;
- ensuring that immigrants have access to services and resources, reviewing provision, and offering services that may be more appropriate to different cultures;
- disseminating adequate information throughout society so that people become more sensitive to these problems, and training workers in statutory and voluntary agencies to take account of these issues;
- promoting and supporting the representation of foreign immigrants.

Efforts are being made to accept diversity and recognize the potential dangers of exclusion: the way is open to co-operate and use all possible resources, and to acknowledge immigrants not just as recipients of help, but as participants in these efforts to improve conditions, and furthermore, to involve all citizens and communities in these efforts. Even if resources can only partially address these problems, it is possible to maximize their effectiveness by co-operation between all those involved. Adult education can, in its various forms, confirm the identity and the capacity for independence of immigrants.

Some current issues

We would like to conclude this section by touching upon some themes that are of concern through all areas of practice.

The problem of compatibility between social work functions of control and of help has been the centre of much attention and debate, both ethically and in respect of the more technical issue of the methodologies to be used. For example, there is a search for an approach that will allow the establishment of a clear relationship between the parties, so that control can be used constructively and clients can feel supported while becoming responsible for themselves.

In 1991, a study group of the National Association of Social Workers prepared a Code of Professional Ethics. The code was approved during the Congress of the Association in 1992 and is being debated amongst its members. Also, some schools of social work and study centres have been experimenting with ways of teaching professional ethics in their curriculum. It is possible that this debate about the nature of social work ethics will develop in the context of a broader debate on the ethics of service organizations and institutions. In the last few years, new legislation and regulations have been introduced aimed at defining appropriate and correct behaviour for employees of public services, the quality of services, and citizens' rights to information and participation in this field.

Another area of research, especially in recent years, identifies problems of stress or burn-out among social workers and other professionals in the health and social services. Alongside specific studies, there have also been studies on social workers' roles, including data on the satisfactions and dissatisfactions of their work. Some indications have emerged concerning the possible causal factors, both of a personal nature and in relation to the organization within which social workers operate.

Other problems which are being debated relate to the management of social services: attempts are being made to define the specific requirements for this role (which is also open to other professionals), and the training needed for it.

More recent developments are in the field of computerization of social services. New technologies, as well as an increasing emphasis on users' rights of access to records and data protection (reaffirmed in recent legislation), have made it necessary to consider in more detail the contents of professional documents and records kept by social workers. Data and assessments need to be confidential, but at the same time they must serve the needs of both users and service planners.

Both central government and local authorities have shown an increased tendency to sign covenants (contracts) with voluntary and non-profitmaking organizations for the management of a variety of personal social services. It is therefore more important than ever to define criteria and methods for the accreditation of such services, and their quality control; it is also increasingly important that citizens should obtain timely and accurate information about eligibility and access to services. Social workers have a significant role to play in all these areas.

Social work education

Basic training

Social work training courses, according to the most recent statutes, are courses of three years' duration, following 13 years of schooling. They aim to prepare 'generalist' social workers, and also to provide homogeneous training standards throughout the country – even though there may be variations in the curriculum in order to harmonize the training with regional social services legislation and with special local needs.

Training courses can be linked with different schools (faculties) in universities, as there is a degree of autonomy in each university. Nevertheless, teaching must comprise at least 1,500 hours, of which not less than 600 must be devoted to practice.

The curriculum includes seven subject areas, of which six are compulsory for all schools of the country:

- professional social work (5 courses of 2 semesters' duration including principles and bases of social work, social policy, methods and techniques in social work and organization of social services);
- psychology (3 courses of 1 semester duration);
- sociology (3 courses of 1 semester duration);
- legislation (3 courses of 1 semester duration);
- public health (2 courses of 1 semester duration);
- economics (1 course of 1 semester duration);
- educational sciences (1 course of 1 semester duration).

The curriculum also demands that each student attend at least six optional courses in different subjects.

Teaching in the areas of methods and techniques in social work examines and discusses processes of helping individuals, and also work with collective dimensions: group work and community work. Courses include an introduction to theoretical social work models, with descriptive presentations of some of them. Regarding the choice of methodology, there is a prevalence in most schools for an integrated, holistic approach, where the knowledge base can be located in systems theory or ecological systems theory, ego psychology and cognitive theory. Different operational strategies can be followed from these frameworks, but in general, the stress is on the educational component of the social work role, rather than on the therapeutic one.

There are some schools, however, where training has its basis mostly in a systemic relational approach, while in other schools networking theory is pre-eminent – both the personal network of users, and the network systems in the community.

In several schools there are problems concerning the relationship between professional subjects and other core subjects. In particular, there is some tension between the teaching of psychology and the teaching of social work methodology. Although efforts are made to relate the one to the other, the subjects are often presented independently. There are also problems concerning discrepancies between the methodology as taught in the school, and what actually happens in practice placements. A process for resolving this problem has been started by formalizing the existing relationship between schools of social work and practice supervisors – for instance, by requiring supervisors to attend qualifying seminars and courses.

Some specific training aims and objectives evident in social work training courses are to:

- place greater attention on users' strengths, their cognitive capacities, and their ability to plan their own future;
- develop a conception of individuals as actors who belong to networks of relationships built by themselves, as bearers of a culture, and as possessing competence in certain skills;
- promote a positive philosophy in which recognized need represents a potential growth point, not necessarily a deficiency;
- contribute a conception of the social work role, whereby the socio-educational components prevail, and where there is an orientation towards planning together with users and towards educational 'partnership' with users;
- give attention to emergent social problems, which represent future challenges within the context of increasing comparison with the standards in other European countries.

A major critical point for the new training is the practical feasibility of ensuring adequate numbers of qualified teachers for professional subjects. Access to such teaching posts is open to people holding a degree, who may not necessarily have any practical or theoretical training in social work. This is because in order to teach in a university setting, it is necessary to have a degree, but there is at present no degree in social work. Recently, some social workers holding a degree in another discipline have been admitted to doctoral studies in sociology and social work methodology; this then qualifies them to teach in schools of social work. At present, pending a more appropriate solution, social workers without a degree but holding a diploma are still teaching in schools of social work, in a precarious situation, as they are all on annual contracts.

Professional practice placements are an integral part of training programmes; they involve work experience within a social work agency, monitored by a social work teacher, who is responsible for the placement, and supervised by the agency supervisor, who implements it. This system is often referred to as 'double tutoring'. The placement is agreed between the school of social work (which defines the objectives and criteria of the training programme) and the agency. It is formalized through an agreement, and based on a project connected with the teaching on professional practice.

The placement does not consist simply of 'operating' (i.e. being a social worker), but includes an opportunity for exploration of the activities undertaken. This allows students to focus on themselves, to develop their conception of their professional roles, and to learn about professional methods. Supervisors attend periodic group meetings as well as having individual contact with the professional methods teachers, and also attend seminars concerning their own role as supervisors. These seminars are being offered with increasing frequency and depth by many schools (e.g. Turin, Venice, Rome, and others). In some areas (e.g. the University of Turin), there is a permanent supervisors' unit, which meets periodically in order to discuss core issues in professional training and practice placement.

There are many innovative practices, concerning both the objectives and the methods in social work education (e.g. research placements). Teaching methodology in schools of social work has traditionally adopted an active, participatory methodology:

● Considerable attention is now given to the small group, where students can confront the issues jointly, and explore their experience together, supporting each other through any emotional problems that arise as a consequence of direct contact with clients.

● Extensive use of simulation is made, both of individual and group meetings – these are video-recorded and critically re-examined.

● Greater use has been made of recent reports or records of social workers, which facilitates understanding by students of suggested theoretical guidelines for practice.

● Various techniques are employed to stimulate and encourage the creativity and originality of future social workers.

● Interdisciplinary seminars are organized on practice issues or techniques of intervention, so that integration between core subjects in the social sciences and professional teaching can be facilitated.

Continuing education: Characteristics and trends

Continuing education is becoming a significant factor in speeding up the process of regeneration of the professional role of social workers. Only now is the need for continuing education being generally recognized by agencies. They provide funding – albeit in different proportions throughout the country – to initiatives suggested by social workers and/or by service managers, and require their workers to attend further compulsory training.

In the last few years, the most frequent themes in continuing education have been methodological aspects of social work, such as analysis of the organization, use of groups, networking, project work, or else particular subjects, such as child abuse, or even exploration of workers' experiences, so that learning can come through experience. There are also several initiatives for updating knowledge about legislation and social policy.

Training is also regarded as an instrument to generate innovation and redefine aspects of professional identity. Some training initiatives are a response to the introduction of new activities, or new problems that have been identified (e.g. in the case of immigrants, AIDS patients, when child abuse became more evident than previously, or when alternative measures to custodial sentences became more common – especially in cases of drug dependency).

Training initiatives are also used as an opportunity to encourage inter-disciplinary co-operation and planning (e.g. training given in the Lombardy region during 1994/95 on alcohol-connected pathologies). In the same way, there have been training initiatives directed to professionals and volunteers jointly, in order to encourage co-operation in dealing with practice problems within a given geographical area and community.

Schools of social work are becoming increasingly involved in this area of continuing education. This is a very positive indication of the change taking place in the relationship between services and schools.

Themes and issues: What future for social work?

At present, the serious economic crisis, an increase in new needs and the per-sistence of 'old poverties' in many areas, an insufficient concern for social needs and problems on the part of policy-makers, and the obvious ambiva-lence of political attitudes towards public services make it difficult to be very optimistic about the profession and the mode of its employment.

There are good reasons to fear that public intervention in the social sector will become increasingly residual, and will concern itself only with basic needs, leaving a much larger role to the voluntary and private, non-profit-making sector. But however creditable and relevant the work of private orga-nizations may be, it does not guarantee the presence of necessary services in all parts of the country, that those services will be of high quality, or that the desired result of interventions will be achieved.

The new legislation and regulations appear to have exhibited some contra-dictions with the general guidelines of the past years, so that the separation between health and social services seems to have been reinstated, with a greater stress on therapeutic intervention and much less emphasis on social prevention. There is a risk that social work may become more bureaucratic and be used more as an agent of social control, rather than for education and empowerment.

The situation is somewhat different with regard to other professions, such as psychologists and the professional *educatori*, who can more easily find their own occupational 'space' as they have less responsibility for social control or crisis intervention. An additional hindering factor in the develop-ment of the social work profession is the fact that it is still often seen as an activity mainly based on dedication and common sense, and not necessarily requiring a professional qualification.

However, there are some significant factors which might have a positive influence on the future of the profession. New synergetic developments can be expected from the relationship between professional associations and the social workers' trade union, and from the relationship between these groups, the schools of social work and the association of social work teachers. Such initiatives should in turn support and render more incisive any action for the development of the profession. In particular, these are likely to focus on:

- relationships which are likely to develop between schools of social work and universities; this should lead to a deeper understanding of special training needs, particularly where the teaching of professional social work subjects is concerned, so that safeguards can be introduced with regard to specific competencies needed for teachers, which again should improve their status;

- relationships between regional authorities and universities, so that a closer relationship between professional educational institutions and organizations employing the professionals may be established;

- possibilities of establishing within the public services a career structure in accord with the professional education and the responsibilities assigned to social workers;

- establishing a constructive relationship with the media in order to pro- mulgate a more positive image of social work;

- developing a more systematic interaction with parallel European struc- tures; at present, these contacts happen in a very limited way, and they are restricted to the experiences of a few schools, or even a few teachers; it is important that these contacts are not reduced to a search for simplistic approaches that could be immediately transferred from one country to another; social workers in the field should also have the opportunity to participate as of right in the international debate.

It will be essential to develop research on practice. Often, original innova- tions take place, but these are rarely publicized. Possibly of even greater importance would be the establishment of a proper observatory where con- tinuous attention could be paid to experiments, allowing effective monitor- ing and dissemination of the findings throughout the country.

The expansion of social work in the private, non-profitmaking sector pre- sents positive opportunities for social work. To date, there has been little discussion on the merits of social work as a focus of private professional practice. The advantages and disadvantages of private practice have not even been discussed in a country where the very identity of social work has been closely linked to public employment. It is possible that since a register for social work has been established, these new prospects may develop. In any case, nobody would wish private practice to become the refuge of practitioners wanting to engage in merely psychotherapeutic or psychological activities, with a higher status and higher fees, directed mainly at the middle class; hopefully, nobody will want to see a reduction in the commitment to the interests of the more disadvantaged groups, or in the resolve to act upon the causes of social exclusion.

Endword

In the 1990s, the production of social work literature has been growing considerably. It is significant that some well-known publishers have started publishing social work series, as is the case with Franco Angeli and the Nuova Italia Scientifica. Besides the publication of books, we must note the wealth of papers concerning projects, research and field experiences which appear only in professional journals; some of them do not actually get printed and remain in the archives of agencies (as is the case for innovative social work practices) or in school of social work libraries (as is the case with the theses students have to write in order to obtain their diploma). In the bibliography for this chapter, we have mainly included books. It has been a difficult choice, particularly bearing in mind that it is addressed to non-Italian readers. It has not been possible to include all the significant texts. We have also tried to include some publications from the 1980s that could help in understanding the development of social work and social work education in Italy.

6 Social work in the Netherlands

Geert van der Laan and Robert Ploem

Translated by Michael Dallas

Introduction

'Social work itself is always bound up with the character of the total society of which it is a part.' So concluded Cooper and Pitts (1994) on the basis of comparative transnational European social work research. They argue that people in different countries think differently. They had envisaged a pilot project to compare the social work role in French and English child protection work. Their original intention was to record how social workers in each country would respond to various presenting problems. But when the British researchers sat down with their French colleagues to design the case study, they discovered that the *systems* were so dissimilar that a case developing in one country quickly takes on features unrecognizable in the other. According to Cooper and Pitts, vocabularies are 'systems of meaning, in which each term finds its place by reference to, and in connection with, other discursively compatible terms. They are internally consistent vocabularies.'

Comparing social work education and social work in the Netherlands with their counterparts in other countries is therefore no easy task. We start by reviewing recent government policy on social welfare and healthcare, and examine its impact on one specific field of practice: general social work in the community. We then outline Dutch social work education, and summarize the main forms of social work practice and the role of the generalist social worker. At the end, we offer a guide to useful sources of information about Dutch social work.

The first school of social work in the Netherlands was founded in 1899, and claims to be the first of its kind in the world. The initiators were progressive bourgeois liberals and social democrats, who felt the need to educate and support working-class people living and working in deprived conditions. Graduates of this school were the first professional social workers, and they devoted themselves chiefly to *advising* and *educating* people in need.

After the Second World War, the emphasis in social work education shifted from teaching students to oversee clients, to a more professional approach. Social and task-oriented casework were introduced. The education and training of social workers acquired a very different focus: *clients' own wishes and needs* became the basic point of reference.

In the 1970s, political analyses of the clients' conditions gained ascendancy at social work schools, and social work institutions came to be branded as oppressive. Social work methods were neglected in some curricula, although new methods were introduced.

Another change in emphasis took place in the 1980s. Education now focuses more strongly on the development and application of methods of social work and care provision, and collaboration with field agencies has been intensified. Schools train students to deal with the problems of client systems in a permanently-changing society, and also provide them with the requisite skills to move on to new target groups such as asylum seekers, homeless psychiatric patients, drug users and prostitutes.

The welfare and health policy context of social work in the Netherlands

The general aims of Dutch welfare policy today are officially presented, by the Ministry of Welfare, Health and Cultural Affairs, as follows:

- mobilizing people;
- stimulating them to participate in society;
- promoting integration and re-integration.

Two large-scale operations now under way are designed to achieve these aims:

1 *Restructuring care and welfare* – This policy seeks to respond more justly to clients' needs and to establish more effective structures of provision.
2 *Social renewal* – The foremost aim of this government campaign is to mobilize citizens who have become sidetracked in unemployment or disability schemes, thereby risking social isolation.

The care restructuring policy has been translated into a number of specific policy interventions. This produces an 'intervention mix' (Van der Laan, 1994a), containing policy initiatives towards:

- de-institutionalization of care;
- care provision structured according to various functions (see below for further discussion);

- introduction of market mechanisms;
- administrative decentralization.

Such measures are intended to relieve the increasing bottlenecks in the care sector.

Interventions are in line with a number of current developments in society and politics:

- the movement to reassess the welfare state;
- the increasing influence of consumer opinion;
- the effort to reduce the distance between citizens and politics.

These factors are set out in Table 6.1, which offers an analysis of the 'intervention mix'.

Table 6.1   Intervention mix

	From facilities to functions	*From centralized to decentralized management*
From institutional to non-institutional	1 Disposition	2 Localization
From bureaucracy to market	3 Alignment	4 Regulation

The two interventions on the left-hand side of the schema in Table 6.1 – de-institutionalization and market orientation – aim to devolve care towards the local community with the objective of containing costs. The two across the top – functional structuring and decentralization – are largely aimed at making services more flexible. Merging these aims together in the four cells of the table yields the following options:

1 *Disposition* – Provision is refocused from 'heavy' to 'light' care, from specialized to generic, from separate hierarchies to linked networks of care. Much-used concepts are: de-institutionalization, individualized care, working programmatically, building specialist networks of agencies and workers ('circuit building'), and substitution. In some fields of practice, reallocation of roles has been coupled with expansion in the size of agencies, enabling one agency to offer several different functions.

2 *Localization* – The central purpose here is to bring care itself, and control over it, closer to the local community. Home care, in the broad sense of the term, is now being provided both by the health services and (to a lesser

extent) by the mental healthcare system. In youth social work, much attention is being centred on various forms of intensive home treatment. We often hear the phrase 'in people's own worlds'. These seem to be focused for the most part at the social micro-level. Management has been partially devolved to local authorities.

3   *Alignment* – This refers mainly to matching supply and demand. Clients' needs are brought into line with consumer demands. Sometimes the latter are also taken to mean the wishes of the agency funding or commissioning the work. Similar conditions apply to insurance firms: they must put together an adequate package at a favourable price to consumers. The idea is that contracts between funders and care providers will guarantee a suitable balance of supply and demand.

4   *Regulation* – This concerns the management of care. The desired trend is from bureaucratic over-regulation to remote manipulation and deregulation. Any further course corrections are to be made mainly by the market. Local authorities seek to influence agreements about care plans between care providers and insurance firms only from a distance. Where public grants are involved, output budgeting is a widely-advocated instrument to induce care providers to carry out policy aims. Quality management is supposed to ensure that the care providers' product lives up to certain standards. Economies of scale are to yield greater efficiency.

Social work practice

The chief difference between the Netherlands and other countries in the field of social work probably lies in the fact that Dutch social work has produced a huge number of specialisms. Examples are sociocultural work, community development, youth work, personnel work, probation work, guardianship, work with Travellers, sociopedagogical work, and social advice work. Statistics covering the entire field of social work and social welfare are hard to track down. In discussing current developments in greater detail, we shall therefore restrict ourselves to the field of generalist community social work (*algemeen maatschappelijk werk* – AMW). The decision to concentrate on one specific field makes it possible to describe developments in some depth. We believe these developments are more or less representative for the whole field of social work and healthcare.

Generalist community social work

Generalist social work in the community is the main area of employment for social workers. It can be briefly characterized as follows, after Van der Laan (1994b).

It is a generalist service at the local level, demand-oriented, available and accessible to all. Because of its position at the interface of care and welfare provision, it reaches especially less-educated, lower-paid people and minorities in Dutch society. Generalist social work focuses on the interdependence between material and non-material problems which impede how individuals function in their environment. Its approach integrates *concrete care and service provision* and *process-oriented guidance,* according to rigorous professional standards. It seeks to provide care that fits as closely as possible with the experiential world of service users, and to speak clients' own language. Generalist social work mainly aims to encourage clients to re-establish their grip on their life situation, so they can take part fully in social life.

Such premises are not free from controversy. Generalist community social work has come under pressure from a complex set of developments. The number of clients has practically doubled within fifteen years, while staff strength has not been expanded in recent years. Choices therefore have to be made. Some agencies opt for groups of people who are most in need. Others try to preserve the broad, generalist nature of social work in the community by soliciting supplementary project grants. Some local authorities are exerting pressure to provide the most concrete and short-term help possible in order to reduce waiting lists. People with severe psychological problems are referred to other agencies when possible, but the Regional Institutes for Out-Patient Mental Health Care (RIAGGs) sometimes promptly send them back. Clients with material problems are referred, when possible, to agencies such as social advice centres, but some of them come back to the social workers if their problems are tied to non-material circumstances.

Registration data confirm that the perceived increase in work pressure has an objective base. Growth in the number of applications for help has not been compensated for by staff expansion (Van der Laan and Potting, 1995). Moreover, research on the *nature* of problems being handled by the more highly-pressured agencies (as in the town of Apeldoorn) indicates that many of their cases are time-consuming ones. On the other hand, a decrease was found in the number of (time-consuming) home visits, and the average number of contacts with each client appears to have declined. Figures from Groningen show, in addition, that an increase in work pressure leads to a lengthening of the average *duration* of provision: contacts are spread out over longer periods. High workload is obviously an elastic phenomenon, manifesting itself in many different local patterns. Agencies and workers try to regulate the pressure in every way they can.

Generalist social work is a basic first-echelon or primary service. Its hallmark is broad accessibility. The appropriateness of the choice to make such services the basis of social work provision is backed up by registration data and other indicators, and since the late 1980s it has received a strategic boost from the devolution of powers to the municipal level. To a greater extent than was the case under centralized control, municipalities call upon social work to deal with problems stemming from poverty, crime, nuisance, social isolation, ageing, unemployment and daily routine, debts and other such conditions. However, the problems enjoying the greatest policy interest are precisely those which consume the largest amounts of time and energy: for example, various co-operative projects relating to case management, debt management, problem families or chronic psychiatric patients. In other words, being at the front line of policy responses costs time and money. Social work must make its own choices in policy as a consequence. We will highlight here two of the many areas in generalist social work where this is the case:

- the choice between material and non-material aid;
- the choice between caring and mobilization.

Material and non-material aid

It looks as though the classic dilemma of social work – the choice between healthcare and welfare work – will remain an issue for the foreseeable future. By extension, so will the choice which is often considered to flow from it: that between a more therapeutic approach directed at non-material problems, and a concrete approach dealing with material matters. The push to segregate the generalist social work function into a 'material' and a 'non-material' stream was set in motion in the 1980s from two different sources.

Given the increase in applications for material aid, some social work agencies decided to devote more attention to *concrete aid*. Especially in the cities, Utrecht and The Hague in particular, part of the available social work staff was deployed in the 1980s in the information and advice aspect of material aid provision. The material stream later received additional impetus from the governmental programme for social renewal, with its emphasis on less care and more concrete aid and mobilization. Some 70 per cent of the municipalities are part of this policy approach. Social renewal is thus set to play a key role, because since the late 1980s, funding and management of social work has been devolved to the municipalities.

There was also another reason for the movement to segregate the material and non-material aspects of social work. In an attempt to survive the turmoil of the restructuring campaign in the field of healthcare and welfare, social work generalists began focusing more on non-material problems – on the 'psychosocial care function' within the system of healthcare funding – as a domain to be claimed by social work. The welfare image was to give way to the health image. These professionals did not encroach on the territory of the social advisers, community welfare workers or information and advice bureaux, as the first movement did, but on that of the RIAGGs and the psychologists in the primary healthcare sector.

Generalist social work in the network of provision

In response to the many attempts to segregate the material and non-material aspects of social work, we have argued in the past that the fundamental concern of social work must be the *interlinkage* between material and non-material problems, and that social work operates at the *interface* of care and welfare. Healthcare and social work have built up a strong tradition of co-operation since the 1970s. General medical practitioners, district nurses and family care workers work together with social workers in many health centres and home teams. Psychosomatic and psychosocial problems are addressed integrally in interdisciplinary teams. These first-echelon teams are intended to act as a filter for referrals to semi-residential and residential somatic and mental healthcare facilities. Problems too severe for primary care are referred to secondary or tertiary care. Conversely, those patients who are considered by higher echelons 'to have been through every therapy' are sent back to primary care. At secondary and tertiary levels, too, social workers are engaged in looking after patients in the social aspects of their illness and after they return home.

In the echelon model, the 'soldiers' at the front are in the first echelon. Given that the term 'echelons' (stepped lines) comes from military strategy handbooks, perhaps more of this soldierly vocabulary will be appropriate. General practitioners, home care officials and social workers would then be the front-line troops. Characteristic of them is their focus on society: they are meant to respond to everything that comes their way, dealing with it themselves whenever possible. That gives them a broad and general panorama. What they are not able to deal with as 'advance guard', they allow through to the more specialized 'rearguard' in the second and third echelons.

Registration figures reveal that the front echelon came under increasing pressure in the course of the 1980s. The number of clients in community social work doubled during that period. What was exceptional was that the front line not only came under pressure from ahead due to increasing demand from society, in effect it was also 'attacked from behind' as a result of the policy of de-institutionalization. In virtually all agency networks in specialist areas (for example, mental health, addiction, older people), this policy touched off a stream of clients moving towards primary care. In spite of efforts to modernize care provision and spread a safety net in primary care services such as home care and reception facilities, the growing number of homeless young people and homeless people with psychiatric problems provides evidence of the unforeseen side-effects of de-institutionalization. Many severe problems are receiving insufficient help. The effect of this, together with general social processes such as individualization and unemployment, causes vulnerable groups to be driven more rapidly towards the margins of society.

The relationship with community development work and sociocultural work

So, in practice, not everything goes according to the manual. For a variety of reasons, for example, many psychiatric patients are not caught by the safety net of primary care, but slip through it (Van der Laan, 1994b). They end up on the streets or being housed in all sorts of care facilities. It is here that the relationship with welfare work comes into view. As generalist social work developed in the Netherlands, it gained independence from community development work and sociocultural work. Their relationship cooled further during the 1980s, when generalist work was orienting itself to healthcare. But in recent years there has been a revival of contact under the influence of decentralization and the social renewal campaign.

Community development work, or community organization, concentrates on issues that go beyond individual interests. It works for safe neighbourhoods, affordable housing, healthy surroundings, a tolerant social climate, afford-able child care, public participation procedures, and jobs for unemployed local people. *Sociocultural work* is distinguished from development work by its focus on individuals' education and self-development. Daily pursuits, recreation and cultural development go hand in hand. Both types of social work are distanced from 'individual care'. By the same token, Dutch generalists have become increasingly specialized in psychosocial care for individuals and families. In this way, these endeavours have drifted apart.

In the early years of welfare work in the post-war period, interventions at micro-, meso- and macro-levels were seen as extensions of one another. In the 1960s, Broekman (1964) distinguished the following methods in social work: individual casework, social group work, community organization and social action. Thus, social work in those days was far less differentiated than it is now.

It would seem that generalist social work has considerably limited its domain in recent decades. In the 1950s and 1960s, the notion of psychosocial care still had broad connotations. In the 1980s it became more or less nar-rowed to *therapeutic aid* to individual applicants with non-material problems. The most promising career opportunities for generalist social workers today lie in specialization in some therapeutic school. People who have no ambi-tions to go into management or teaching but wish to develop their skills in practical social work have little incentive to choose a broad orientation rather than a specialized one.

Although recently a new career perspective has dawned at the opposite end of the spectrum – social rights services – specialization is still the trend for further career development. There are few prospects in the 'hazy' border-line areas, and especially not in a concentration on the link between material and non-material problems. The material side in particular seems to have fallen out of favour. Debt management has been relegated to a lower status within community social work than psychosocial care. This is reflected in the level of education for it at the lower-level vocational colleges (see below).

Several causes can be cited for this trend: the introduction of national assistance in the mid-1960s, the rapid expansion of all kinds of interesting therapeutic techniques in the 1970s, and the re-organization of the care sector in the 1980s. In the 1963 National Assistance Act, the government under-wrote the basic living expenses of those who could not fend for themselves. Some 750,000 people (5 per cent of the population) are currently receiving benefit under this scheme. The need to provide material help through gener-alist community social work was thus diminished by the assistance scheme, causing attention to shift to the non-material side. This trend was strength-ened in the 1980s as social workers jockeyed for a place under the health legislation. Influenced in part by the 'New Realism', generalist social work turned away from welfare work, made overtures to the healthcare sector, and tried to secure a position under the 'psychosocial care function'. In this way, a gradual, more or less unnoticed process has been under way for decades in which the term 'psychosocial' has come to stand for 'therapeutic'. The broad definition it had borne since the generation of Kamphuis, one of the pioneers of social casework in the Netherlands, has been narrowed. The 'rehabilita-tion' function has been squeezed out of the picture to some extent. Restoring the balance may not pose many problems, but methodological, theoretical and ideological obstacles will have to be removed first.

It must be acknowledged that a number of gaps have appeared in general-ist social work. Meanwhile, some of them have been filled by activities such as social advice services, work with marginal groups, and social psychiatric nursing; others still lie open, awaiting new initiatives.

The broad-based function of generalist community social work

From research findings and registration figures in community social work, an image emerges of a field of practice that reaches the lower-educated and lower-paid of society. Because community social work holds a rather solid 'market position' among this group, the use of this service is not subject to sharp fluctuations. Over the years it has exhibited a steady pattern which plainly distinguishes it from other fields. Registration data reflect a strong interdependency between material and non-material problems. Further-more, they show that the use of community social work follows the major trends in society (Van der Laan, 1995). When unemployment rises, so does the number of unemployed people on client registers, as a result of financial problems and the like. The same is true of, for example, rising divorce rates, percentages of people living alone or immigration. Some social tendencies show up disproportionately for certain population traits, like national origin, while other trends, such as 'greying' (the ageing of the population), seem to have less impact on community social work, probably because separate modes of provision exist for them.

Caring or mobilization

The position of generalist social work at the interface between care and welfare, discussed above, is not only a theoretical concern. It has practical consequences. It means that social work sometimes has a caring nature, and sometimes a mobilizing one; or both aspects can operate simultaneously, so that the residual capabilities of the clients are tapped. General principles like social re-integration, rehabilitation and probation and prison aftercare have historically occupied a central place in social work. The tension between caring and mobilization makes itself felt in many sectors of generalist social work. In a recent study on the care of clients with employment disabilities, Melief (1994) found that social workers generally offer good-quality care when it comes to *retrospective* matters – this refers to emotional elements (providing a listening ear, showing understanding, and giving encouragement) as well as to rational–cognitive elements (creating order and seeking causes). However, the more *future-* and *action-oriented* elements come off rather poorly. Stimulating clients to make concrete plans for the future and helping them build a new repertoire of behaviour receive comparatively little attention. Moreover, as Melief observes, many concrete, practical aspects of the problem situation 'come up less in the counselling the further away they lie from the consulting room'.

According to Melief, generalist community social work is too strongly oriented to the past and too inward-directed. Especially for clients who, for whatever reasons, are out of work, an outward-directed and future-oriented view is called for. Many clients are in danger of sinking into passivity, and a mobilizing approach is therefore essential to keep alive the prospect of renewed social participation.

If we observe from a distance the Dutch discussion on mobilizing welfare work, we see it is dominated by a limited number of oppositions. The most important of them are juxtaposed in Table 6.2 (see also Engbersen & Van der Laan, 1995).

Encouraged by the change in policy, the centre of gravity now lies mostly on the options in the right-hand column of Table 6.2. Sometimes this shows up in practices which open new horizons; sometimes it is no more than lip service to policy. Some workers may translate terms on the left into those on the right. The first pair of concepts is a good example. Forms of care (feeding and clothing someone, and helping them calm down and come to their

Table 6.2   The poles of care and mobilization

Care	Mobilization
Dependency	Self-reliance
Solidarity	Individual responsibility
Social causes	Personal causes (individual failures)
Thinking in terms of problems	Thinking in terms of potentials
Reluctance to intervene (fear of being patronizing)	Eagerness to intervene ('stepping in')
Retrospective	Prospective
Introspective	Action-oriented

senses) could be represented as the first step on the route to mobilization. The mobilization paradigm promises to be a key factor in generalist social work in the years to come. By applying techniques from methodologies like task-centred casework, social workers try to give form to a mobilizing approach in individual counselling.

In summary, we think that generalist social work in the Netherlands has become somewhat alienated from its historical roots in recent years. It has concentrated too much on therapy and on its clients' non-material existence. It needs to re-orient itself towards its classic task: improving the social participation of vulnerable groups in society.

Social work education in the Netherlands

In recent decades, social work has been taught at the level of higher professional education (*hoger beroepsonderwijs* – HBO), which awards the degree of *ingenieur*. In principle, graduates are entitled to go on to study for a university doctorate in social science. However, since they acquire few research skills as yet in the schools of social work, they have difficulty competing with university graduates applying for doctorate courses, and are rarely admitted. Higher professional education in the Netherlands trains students not only to perform a full range of professional duties in social work practice, but also to contribute to policy-making in their agencies, and to the development of the profession as a whole.

In the late 1980s, post-HBO courses in social work were reduced from two-year part-time programmes to one-year part-time intensive courses. This was a result of government privatization of such programmes, which also raised the fees for students from 650 to around 10,000 guilders a year. The certificate can be recorded in a national register. The number of students has now ebbed to 650 per year nation-wide. One type of social work is taught at the upper secondary vocational (MBO) level: community services. This is a three-year practical course.

Although social work is mainly taught at colleges of higher professional education (*hogescholen*), there are two university chairs of social work. One, a chair in Community Development, has existed for several years at Erasmus University in Rotterdam, and last year a chair in Social Work and Community Services was established by the Marie Kamphuis Foundation at Utrecht University.

In the late 1980s and early 1990s, some 400 institutes of higher professional education were operating in the Netherlands. The Dutch government embarked on an amalgamation policy aimed at the formation of large, multi-faculty institutions. Most of the now remaining 25 social work schools are part of such institutions of higher professional education, which are known as *hogescholen*. The number of social work students is still growing, and totalled about 34,000 in 1993/94 (10,000 part-time and 24,000 full-time students). Programmes of social work education have been evaluated by independent review committees (*visitatie commissies*) in recent years. So far, most of them have received satisfactory assessments of the quality of instruction. Only the programmes in cultural and social education met with strong criticism.

The Dutch system of student grants has come under heavy pressure. The system introduced in the 1980s, which provided money for every student over 18 years, has been very successful at attracting students. The government recently limited funded participation in higher professional and university education to five years, and a further reduction to four years has been proposed. Students are given a basic grant amounting to less than 600 guilders (in 1994/95), and they may be eligible for low-interest loans, depending on their parents' income. They are further granted a nation-wide public transport card valued at 60 guilders a month; they may choose either weekday or weekend validity. Cuts are anticipated in the near future, and all higher education institutions (universities and *hogescholen*) will face cutbacks of up to 25 per cent in the coming years. For ten years, higher education institutions have been permitted to take on commissioned work at market prices. Such projects are mainly in the areas of service management, development of practice methods and staff development.

In the past three years, job opportunities for social work graduates have been reasonably stable: one year after graduation, 73 per cent have a paid job, 14 per cent are enrolled in an advanced course of study, 5 per cent are involved in other activities and 9 per cent are still looking for a job.

Developments in social work education

In 1989, the Higher Education in Social and Community Work Sector (*Hoger Sociaal Agogisch Onderwijs* – HSAO) of the Association of Dutch Polytechnics and Colleges (HBO-Raad) ordered the re-organization of social work education, reducing the number of degree programmes to six, reflecting the main service divisions within social work.

1 *Social work and community services (MWD)* – Students are trained here to perform generalist social and task-oriented casework, based on analysis of client systems in their overall social context.

2 *Social and pedagogical work (SPH)* – This trains students to work in residential care services and youth social work. The focus of the curriculum is on therapeutic modes such as play, music, sport and drama.

3 *Cultural and social education (CMV)* – Emphasis is on cultural awareness and development, and basic education for all. Students learn to apply media such as film, music, video and photography as educational tools.

4 *Arts therapy* – Students learn to provide care and therapy using art forms such as drama, painting, music and gardening.

5 *Personnel and labour relations (PenA)* – Students are trained in personnel recruitment and in development and implementation of personnel policy within organizations.

6 *Social rights services (SJD)* – Half the curriculum is devoted to knowledge of the law and its applications, which prepares students to acquaint clients with their legal position. The other half fosters attitudes and skills which enable the social worker to build a help-oriented relationship with clients. This new field of social work is designed to fill the gap between lawyers and social workers.

The professional degree course in social work is four years long. Two different modes of study are offered: *full-time* and *concurrent*.

In the full-time curriculum, students first receive two years of instruction, usually including short field placements. In the third year, they arrange a ten-month fieldwork placement four days a week, while attending a limited number of workshops and lessons at school. Also, they receive 18–20 tutorial and supervisory sessions in groups of two or three, to integrate field experiences, theory and method effectively with students' personal experiences and qualities. In their fourth year, students resume full-time instruction and write a short dissertation.

In the concurrent model, before beginning their studies, students are required to find a field placement or paid job in social work practice for at least 18 hours per week. They attend school concurrently one-and-a-half days a week for four years. This model gives students the greatest possible opportunity to practise the theory and methods taught at school. In the third year, they receive an equal amount of supervision and tutoring to that of full-timers.

Endword: Elements of social work practice and services

A summary of the curriculum in social work and community services is given here as an example of the scope of the most general form of social work, used to qualify workers for generalist community social work discussed above.

The basic programme contains all general and theoretical subjects relating to the profession, requisite general knowledge for understanding the more specific context and background of the profession and professional action, as well as the social contexts and backgrounds of clients and client systems. The fundamental tasks of the social worker are listed as:

1   *Psychosocial care* in a socio-economic, historical and cultural context; inter-dependency of material and non-material problems;
2   *Concrete assistance and information* – short-term advice and assistance; information provision relating to laws, regulations and rights; longer-term assistance such as shelter, guidance, legal and financial aid;
3   *Research and reporting* – researching with clients their social situation; reporting to and advising services, authorities and politicians;
4   *Identification, advocacy and prevention* – pinpointing structural defects in society; informing client groups and representing them to policy-makers; prevention;
5   *Co-ordination of care and assistance* – case management in the interest of clients and client systems; knowledge of networks of the client system, of the social worker and of the professional field agency.

Organizational skills teaching offers what a student needs to know to function in a professional organization. It includes: the formulation of objectives and working methods; the structure of organizations; policy development, and one's own role as a professional. Fieldwork experience placements offer students opportunities to put all the acquired skills and knowledge into practice.

Modern social work in the Netherlands is divided into six areas, each with its own training.

Social and community services work is the oldest and most firmly established kind of social work. Professionals with a Diploma in Social Work and Community Services can join the National Association of Social Workers (Landelijke Vereniging van Maatschappelijk Werkers – LVMW). This organization has developed its own Professional Profile and Professional Social Work Code, setting out the domain of the social worker, and ethics and moral guidelines for its members. Graduates work in many areas, including generalist community social work, probation and aftercare, child protection, guardianship, general and psychiatric hospitals, and political asylum.

Arts therapy is the most therapeutic form of social work. Drama, painting, sculpture, music and gardening are used to explore clients' past and present experiences. These are often combined with intensive treatment in psychiatric hospitals, therapeutic communities or intensive therapeutic daycare centres.

Cultural and social education emphasizes education and training. It is practised in community and youth centres, in sociocultural training and day release centres, and in job-pool centres. The focus is on learning and re-education. Video, film, photography, music and drama may be employed.

Personnel and labour relations focuses on personnel policy and the labour market, and on staffing and recruitment policy. It qualifies students for careers as personnel officers in firms and service institutions. It is considered by its students to be the 'toughest' and most 'businesslike' branch of social work, and they often wish not to call themselves social workers.

Social and pedagogical work combines the former 'residential social work' and 'youth social work', and is still concerned with residential care and services, and with social work with young people. There is a strong focus on learning and living in groups.

Social rights services is a newly-developed mode of social work, having only recently been recognized by the Education Ministry. It is strongly oriented to law, which comprises 50 per cent of the curriculum. It aims to address the growing complexity of society. Their training as care workers enables graduates to supplement the work of lawyers.

We can thus see that there are a range of social work services enabling the skills of social workers to be deployed in a variety of ways. We have identified many constraints as a result of policy and educational changes in the last decade. None the less, social work continues to play a valid and valuable role in Dutch society.

7 Social work in Portugal

Fernanda Rodrigues and Alcina Monteiro

Introduction

Social work is closely linked with welfare provision generally, so this analysis covers both general and specific aspects of social provision and social work in Portugal over the last twenty-five years. During this period, Portugal has been going through changes which are both similar to and different from those in other European countries. Change occurred faster and out of step with trends in other countries.

The Portuguese state did not legally acknowledge its role as a central social provider until the early 1970s. Its role has traditionally been residual, so, until then, the main initiative fell to private, non-profitmaking agencies and organizations. The trend to develop a welfare state grew stronger in Portugal just at the time it declined elsewhere. A recent focus on individualism and privatization in many countries contrasts with the Portuguese debate about achieving provision based on the state, collective and public involvement.

When the political regime changed in 1974, social policy trends to give priority to defending working-class interests (recognizing inequalities between citizens) and improving living conditions (recognizing inadequate structures) were enshrined in the Constitution. Measures announced at the time included diverse areas such as an integrated system of social security, protection schemes for maternity, child care, accidents at work and occupational illnesses, and the foundations of a national health service. A month after the regime changed, the minimum wage was introduced for employees in industry, services and commerce (Law 217/74 of 27/5/74). However, these changes did not result in state intervention and private initiatives becoming separate. Instead, an agreed co-existence between the state and civil society still continues to this day.

The policy context of social provision in Portugal

Santos (1990) argues that Portugal is at an intermediate stage of development, both economically and in its social legislation. Weak state welfare provision is combined with a strong welfare society (that is, support for a caring
society by the population). Although part-funded by the state (about 80 per
cent of their resources originate from state sources) the 2,500 *instituições
particulares de solidariedade social* (IPSS) cover some 90 per cent of the services
and directly provide 35,000 jobs. This includes the 400 exceptionally large
misericórdias. Provision administered through formal agencies is supple-
mented by 'mutual information and self-help networks based on kinship
and neighbourhood for small-scale trade in goods and services on a non-
commercial and reciprocal basis, comparable with the gift relationship
studied by Marcel Mauss' (Santos, 1991, p.37). As a result, two patterns of
welfare exist in an inadequate and incomplete welfare state. First, inter-class
transfers of resources from richer to poorer arise from traditional charitable
giving by philanthropic groups. Second, intra-class transfers derive from
relationships between those who share identical difficulties (Rodrigues,
1995).

The welfare society deals with risk on a day-to-day basis of coping strategies, not legal rights. Citizens' rights are therefore not guaranteed. Also,
current trends are changing and weakening provision through the welfare
society. Portugal shares these characteristics with other Southern European
countries. Their welfare identity has a shared history, in which the Church
played a significant role, public funding is only recent and limited, people are
unaware of and have not internalized their idea of having social rights, and
commercial provision of social care is weak. Such countries also traditionally
have a centralized state. There is an insecure labour market, with low wages
and poor social security. Flexibility, when it appears, tends to imply precarious employment. There is limited recognition of poverty and social
exclusion (Estivill, 1992).

Portugal can be seen as a welfare *system* with mixed provision and minority state provision, rather than as a social welfare state (Gould, 1993). Expenditure on social security in Portugal, as elsewhere in Southern Europe,
represented less than 20 per cent of GDP in 1993. In Central Europe, it was
around 30 per cent.

Portugal has been late in establishing legal and political democracy and
rights to welfare provision. Such rights are limited in effectiveness because
there are no guarantees or universal state care. Instead, there is a mixture provision originating from both the state and civil society. Recent welfare history
has several phases. From 1974, as social provision and its management was
democratized, the state became a funder as well as a (limited) provider.
Redistributive policies became more important using employment measures

or direct payments, as well as through social policy and indirect welfare payments. In the early 1980s, at the same time as preparations were being made for membership of the European Economic Community, social rights were progressively devalued. A market philosophy for goods and services became influential. Portugal's membership of the EEC led to existing social provision being reappraised and reshaped, although its level remained low.

During these periods, the relationship between legal frameworks and political and government practices and the actual extent of social rights must be examined. Considerable legislative progress has given Portugal an advanced legal framework. However, this legislation has not been fully implemented, so guaranteed rights are insufficient, and legal measures are often discredited as empty promises implemented arbitrarily. The Council for Economic and Social Co-operation was set up in late 1986, and the second revision of the Constitution (1989) followed other countries by removing obstacles to privatization in economic and social policy.

Portugal's growth rate has recently been higher than the European Union average, but it remains one of the least prosperous countries in the EU. There was a period of economic development between 1986 and 1991, and of recession between 1992 and 1994. In 1990, GDP per head was 53 per cent of the EU average – one justification for European aid, which contributed about 3.5 per cent to GDP between 1989 and 1993. But if 'economic growth and the creation of greater wealth appears to be the necessary condition of continued and sustained improvement in social welfare, it is certainly not a sufficient condition, especially for the least advantaged' (Ferreira, 1994). Unemployment figures (confirmed by various Portuguese agencies) have reached levels which were formerly unusual, and are still increasing. Recession has led to a consensus that unemployment and social exclusion are important problems facing social policy today. There has been debate about the crisis of the welfare state and the hope of 'salvation' through privatization of social services.

Portuguese social policy is among the least-developed in the European Union, with limited measures in force, and little attention being paid to new areas of concern. Social security, for example, is based on occupation and is strongly influenced by a conservative and corporatist philosophy. It therefore provides unequal coverage and fails to protect some population groups or to guarantee a minimum income. Priorities for reforming this system are the need to identify funding responsibilities, especially in a country with very limited resources, the need to reduce social insurance expenditure, and the need to strengthen provision based on solidarity. The Portuguese system must find harmony between its origins and its recent history. Modern acquisitions are only incompletely incorporated, so that it is simultaneously experiencing both a crisis and a consolidation of the welfare system.

The effects of globalization in economic relations also need attention. The field of economics dominates social thought strongly, whereas the powerlessness of political control over the economy has never been so clear. Recent policy trends in agriculture and fisheries, for example, devalue the family economic model which has provided economic and social equilibrium. Despite globalization, modern societies generate many locally-based initiatives, rooted in local communities. Investment in local development has reshaped intervention according to a vision which integrates the social and economic, political and cultural initiatives, following both macro-policies and guidelines at municipal level. Such an approach seeks to renegotiate the relevance of particular local factors and the contribution they make in mitigating the dominant process of social homogenization. Many local initiatives have emerged in Portugal, virtually all concerned with activities to improve living and working conditions for local people. They offer a platform to link multiple policies, sectors, social dimensions and social actors. This new style of local intervention has involved social work professionals, who have often played a central role in stimulating and driving forward these local movements. However, the potential of locally-based initiatives must be set against persistent obstacles to decentralization.

Social work practice

The policy, political and economic context discussed above influenced the development of professional social work and the social services in Portugal.

Changes in the characteristics of social problems accompany persistent, long-standing social issues, mainly arising from socio-economic inequality. These reappear in new forms because a fragile and dependent society and economy must cope with the economic and social restructuring currently in progress. Social work is thus affected by a combination of new and old problems with old and new methods of intervention. There are demands to search out new ways to overcome long-standing political and service failings. Social workers therefore combine conventional interventions, dealing with persistent problems, with interventions based on newly-developing issues which are still being clarified. This raises the risk of divisions among professionals and within services, and public devaluation of social work professionals, together with their own disillusionment. New problems and approaches may attract more attention professionally, and in political and social discourse. The problem is to avoid devaluing 'old' problems and approaches when focusing on current priorities.

In both welfare and social development, social workers have developed programmes which have strengthened the acceptance and recognition of welfare rights. This has extended the value of citizenship, and has fulfilled the 'old' promise of a welfare state and the 'new' promise of a more pluralist 'welfare society'. At the same time, social workers may restrict themselves to providing individualized assistance according to established policy and practice, and fail to use the opportunity to develop innovative projects. Although Portugal has extensive needs, every initiative is not valid. Projects should be selected which respond to more than one dimension, offering both solutions and preventive strategies achieving lasting change at different levels of intervention, for example with individuals, households and local communities.

Social workers in Portugal are mainly involved in the following policy areas:

- social security;
- employment, work and professional training;
- the courts and social rehabilitation;
- education;
- health and housing;
- local authorities and local action.

Each of these is considered more fully below. Policy developments in responding to poverty, education and local action are considered in more detail, to show how the role of social work is affected by and influences changes in the organization and policy context of social issues.

Social security

Most Portuguese social action initiatives are in social security, because this field has most directly inherited conventional support and social protection measures. Social security is organized into contributory and non-contributory systems, including social action on welfare rights. The long-standing relationship between social action and unemployed people has increasingly been questioned by people who are partly or completely excluded from the social security system, as this has become more precarious and the risks covered more limited.

Providing financial help and facilitating the provision of other material assistance is urgent and important. However, social workers have emphasized the importance of united social action, and social service agencies have developed local development projects focused on anti-poverty initiatives, supported by European Union finance and policy. Multi-agency approaches involving co-operation between central and local authorities and formal projects linked with informal resources such as parents, neighbours and friends have improved knowledge of the problems and effective responses.

Instituições particulares de solidariedade social (IPSSs), with various legal and institutional bases (*misericórdias*, co-operatives, and associations) played an important role in developing social policies to improve social security provision. Portuguese government subsidies contribute about 68 per cent of total social security costs to these social action projects (Social Security Accounts, 1990). These involve the education of children and young people, and the care of elderly people, where informal family contributions are becoming less important. State care funding priorities require IPSS social facilities, such as creches, day nurseries, activity and leisure support centres, day and social centres, domiciliary services, and education and social centres, to focus on providing access for less well-off groups of the population. IPSSs are widespread in many parts of the country, unlike alternative direct state provision. However, many are bureaucratic and paternalistic organizations based on traditional philanthropy. Marginalized social groups may therefore lose opportunities for self-development, as funding directed in this way limits co-operative, participative structures.

Social workers are responsible for managing projects and centres, and also intervene to protect children and young people where poor environments mean that they are at risk of abuse or neglect. An important social work role is mediating between individual needs and agency provision, making services more flexible and identifying new needs. IPSSs increasingly recruit qualified social workers, thus improving the professionalism and quality of their provision. The complexity and extent of the problems associated with poverty, helping marginalized groups adapt to general economic and social development, have led to a variety of measures under the aegis of the Department of Social Action, including the following:

- *For families and communities* – social care and emergency services; support facilities, including night shelters, reception centres and residential care homes, community dining rooms, bathhouses and washhouses; local action projects organized directly and/or through co-operation with other providers.

- *For children and young people* – nursing services and family creches; kindergartens and free-time activities; residential care for children and young people.

- *For disabled people* – technical aids; domiciliary support.

- *For elderly people* – family reception; domiciliary support; support in residential placements in profitmaking and non-profitmaking initiatives; day centres and community centres.

There are about 600 social workers employed in this work across the country.

Employment, work and professional training

Various government agencies and non-profitmaking private organizations work in this field. Intervention seeks to promote employment, self-employment, and to encourage searching for jobs. Social work agencies facilitate identification of local needs and access to information, financial and technical assistance and other resources. Helping unemployed people deal with a complex bureaucratic system and with feelings of hopelessness requires considerable skill, and basic and advanced courses have grown up to cover this field.

Companies and trade unions have developed programmes providing support to students, workers or relatives with special difficulties, retirement pension supplements and invalidity benefit. Social workers have provided management for these programmes, various workplace social services and health and safety activities. Economic restructuring and its effects on large companies has led to help for staff mobility and early retirement packages. As unemployment rates have risen and labour-intensive industries have declined, trade union and other initiatives have promoted training and employment projects, using their own resources and external support. Some social workers have been involved in assessment, follow-up and retraining within such initiatives.

Attempts at social development in the 1970s led to a growing need for professional qualifications, which are less readily available than in much of the European Union. Regional development plans and community support networks have focused on this need, supported by European programmes such as Horizon, Euroform and Now, and national initiatives or support from the Institute of Employment and Professional Training (IEFP). Social workers contributed to dealing with difficulties which arose because marginalized people were not well enough prepared to take up opportunities for professional training, and were likely to drop out, or fail. Also, training focused on industry or commercial needs, rather than developing broad social skills among students. Social work has focused on better preparation for return to or starting work, including better social integration, mediating links between training and suitable jobs, and building networks which allow professionals and trainees to exchange experience at national and European levels. Much of the work has been through information and vocational guidance centres, job clubs and psychosocial support agencies. This work employs about 35 social workers in public agencies, out of a total of 100 involved in all the initiatives.

The courts and social rehabilitation

Prison system and wider penal reforms, introduced in 1979 and 1982 respectively, turned imprisonment into a period of social training, developing offenders' relationships and occupational skills, and counteracting lack of skills and multiple social stigmas. Both prisons and external agencies were encouraged to develop social and educational projects. Social aspects of offenders' situations, including socio-economic and cultural causes of offending and social measures for rehabilitation, were introduced into the criminal justice system.

Among the developments were the following:

- the Institute of Social Rehabilitation (created by Law 319 of 11/8/82) which seeks to establish alternatives to prison, especially for young offenders;
- the Juvenile Court, focused on family and social environments of offenders, including school and neighbourhood relationships, to ensure that adequate support for personal and social development is achieved;
- the Family Court, for adoption procedures, paternity suits and regulation of parental authority.

Social workers are involved in assessment within complex situations with potential stigmas affecting offenders, linking to ensure co-operation and mutual support for rehabilitation within, outside and between agencies, and in designing and organizing follow-up plans. They require training in analytical skills based in several social science disciplines, focusing on problems of marginalization and agency and local resources. Work on altering individual, family and local behaviour and lifestyles as well as agency policies and practices is crucial. About 350 professionals work in this sector.

Health and housing

Health and housing are the responsibility of different political and agency structures, but serious gaps in provision and the close connection between them make it necessary to consider them in relation to one another.

Social work has long been involved in the health field, initially in hospitals, but increasingly in primary care. Preventive medicine, infant mortality rates and life expectancy at birth have all improved as a result of medical advances and stronger social investment. However, progress is unequal across the country and different social groups, and this is closely related to the level of economic and social development. Less-accessible, less-developed regions are more deprived of health resources, and poorer groups receive limited benefit from existing measures and services. During the 1980s, health policy shifted to privatization and marketization of goods and services, and the system became polarized. Reform in the 1990s led to a two-tier system, with state services (mainly basic services which cannot be made profitable) for the socially and economically vulnerable, and a private sector partly sustained by supplying services on contract to the state sector.

Professional health functions are being re-organized along the following lines:

- more emphasis on primary care provided by the state, with greater specialization in responses to new health issues, such as new risks or groups with new problems;
- more interdisciplinary work as prevention and treatment become more complex and developing healthy lifestyles becomes more important;
- involving a wider range of agencies, including service users, citizens and local communities.

Social workers' involvement is about 60 per cent in health treatment as opposed to prevention. Multi-disciplinary work focuses on humanizing services and trying to treat patients as whole persons rather than diagnosed diseases. There is participation in local projects campaigning on health education projects, encouraging participation in health planning through identifying needs and resources and the health element of integrated local development projects. Developing interest groups for particular problems or situations, through organizing volunteers or forming patient or user associations, is another important area of social work. The range and constantly-changing nature of the area has led to post-graduate, specialized training initiatives, including in-service study. Between 400 and 500 professionals are employed in this sector.

Portugal suffers from a serious shortage of housing: 500,000 new houses are needed, and 300,000 houses need major repairs. This affects many of the most vulnerable groups, and even young people whose families of origin are quite well-off. Social housing is mostly provided by local authorities, but resembles ghettos. It has poor architecture, social groups suffering from multiple deprivation are concentrated in particular areas, and social housing is visibly abandoned and stigmatized. Moving from a role in allocating and managing housing, social services have responded to deteriorating conditions by wider involvement. Social workers have organized social, educational and cultural initiatives to combat poor physical environments, encouraged local community development projects aimed at improving living and housing conditions, and promoted employment and professional training. These projects also encourage social contact, participation and self-help organizations. The professional approach combines concern for physical and architectural considerations with social improvement. It seeks to assess and understand the process of impoverishment of the environment and population, to develop material, cultural and professional resources among residents to try to respond to the scale of the problems, and to achieve co-operation among the various professionals involved.

Developments in policy and organization, and the role of social work

The incomplete development of the Portuguese social welfare system has required active involvement in social development at the policy level as well as welfare help to specific individuals and groups, which was the main approach as social work emerged. The countless difficulties and the powerlessness resulting from inadequate living and working conditions among marginalized groups has required intervention, but social workers in Portugal have faced the challenge of contributing to achieving adequate levels of social welfare which have never been reached. Whereas in other countries there has been a stage of disenchantment and dismantling of welfare systems, and social work has sought to resist such moves, in Portugal social work has tried to invest in socio-economic development measures.

For our detailed analysis of services, therefore, we will focus on areas of work which show both individual work with specific groups in need, and work at the policy level. This approach follows that of the Council of Europe (1965), which distinguished two aspects of social work: direct assistance through intervention in concrete problems, and influence on policy measures. These form a dual mandate for social work.

For many years to come, social services in Portugal will mainly be concerned with direct intervention:

- among groups of the population which receive little attention, such as the unwaged, those applying for various goods and services, migrants and those dependent on residential care;
- involving people in developing and creating policies for social services;
- mediating more effective communication between people in need and the local and central authorities.

At the same time, there will be an important focus on achieving lasting changes with broad effects on people in need of social services, by influencing policy.

We shall deal with the following policy areas: poverty, education and local action.

Poverty

Carlos de Oliveira, a famous Portuguese writer, described the Portuguese population as: 'poor children of a poor mother'. An intimate and daily relationship with poverty over decades, together with a low awareness of social and individual rights, has bred complacency about its endemic character.

Poverty can almost be said to be nationalized and normalized. Concern about poverty rose before and after the political change of 1974. Official recognition of the need to promote greater equality grew, and economic development was, at first, seen as the answer. The Survey of Household Income and Expenditure for 1973–74 (Costa et al., 1985) showed that Portugal had a high rate of poverty: 45.7 per cent in the urban environment, and 43.5 per cent in rural areas. Most affected were agricultural workers, small and medium-sized rural proprietors, rural workers and service employees. More recent data made possible by a more favourable political climate show that poverty and social exclusion affect a high percentage of the population (20–25 per cent). Of the Portuguese poor, 53 per cent are retired people, and 35 per cent are economically active. This suggests that for many, wages only cover minimum subsistence expenditure – and very insecurely at that. The same applies to people on social security benefits: 70 per cent of Portuguese pensioners receive less than 50 per cent of the national minimum wage – less than 140 ECU per month. Although unemployment is low compared with the European average, about 60 per cent of unemployed people and 95 per cent of young unemployed people do not receive unemployment benefit. Unemployment benefit is on average below the minimum wage, currently 54,700 escudos (280 ECU).

'Given the high percentage of poor people in the country and the unequal distribution by age and area of the processes of impoverishment and social exclusion across the country, there are many areas where the majority of the local population can be regarded as poor and excluded' (Rodrigues and Henriques, 1994). There are 'pockets' of poverty where it is concentrated, but it is a structural problem, combining 'old' and 'new' features.

Poverty and social exclusion were disregarded in political debate, social priorities and academically, except for the enduring connection of social work with this issue. Since qualified intervention was felt to be needed, poverty was an important factor in social work's emergence. Social workers are the only professional group with really systematic links among those living on the margins of society. The 'rationalization' of assistance to the poor has been so intertwined with social work's existence that Netto (1990) says: 'the profession arises less from an already formulated theoretical status than from the way in which social issues determine the intervention of the public authorities'. Its close relationship with the practical has elevated its application above any theoretical and academic basis. The practical has been separated from the theoretical in a dichotomy which has been only recently questioned with attempts to value the unity of theoretical and practical knowledge of poverty. Poverty is not easily tolerated, especially where Catholic morality is socially important and alternatives exist to much of the standard state provision, although the philosophy of the alternative provision is minimalist.

For a long time, professional practice regarded the individual as the cause of poverty, and regarded the poor as the only people who could solve their problems. However, the developmentalist movement has undermined this view and promotes a view that global economic and social development is needed to overcome local poverty. As a result, a need was perceived to develop social policy separately from economic growth, which does not generally reduce social inequalities. Social work interventions began to include promotional and co-operative practices. Developments such as social promotion and family co-operation services go beyond multi-disciplinary intervention and seek joint agency initiatives targeting particularly destitute areas. Such approaches move from dealing with poverty on an individual basis, and relocate social work as an agent of organizational strategies to promote locally-based action.

Since 1974, government programmes have treated poverty as a policy area, although responses were variable. In 1980, the government announced the 'war on poverty', influencing official awareness, but also leading to increasing public criticism of the extent of poverty in Portugal (Rodrigues et al., 1988). More recently, European Union programmes have stimulated measures to combat poverty, providing housing and employment training. Social workers have been key professionals in the design, implementation and evaluation of these projects. This created or strengthened a professional attitude which Jean-Marie Barbier described as 'a civilization of projects'. In action against poverty, project-based work is unusual because the typical approach had been agency interventions with individuals and families. These projects, therefore, have particular characteristics.

- They focus on new local organizations rather than, or as well as, state and philanthropic organizations and traditional 'solidarity initiatives'.
- They encourage an environment for social innovation.
- They help connect theoretical and practical knowledge for workers.
- Linking anti-poverty action with development is unconventional, and runs counter to accepted practice and policy which fragment professional and policy work.

One significant outcome of poverty projects based on different contexts and a variety of social players has been to counter piecemeal and oversimplified understanding of problems. For example, social policies compartmentalize multi-faceted human needs, and so have difficulty in promoting development. Additional financial resources are needed, and are particularly important in countries such as Portugal for connections between social action and development to highlight new directions. As the complexity of poverty and the multiple agencies and contexts that must be involved emerges, classic dichotomies between economic and social causes are challenged. As a result, we can better understand how social policies can influence local action, even in the context of global competitiveness. This crossover between economic and social policies has lately involved many social workers. It leads in the direction of a new role for the state. The recent White Paper on European social policy explicitly refers to this role as finding ways of empowering solidarity and competitiveness together (European Commission, 1994).

Certain principles arising from such projects are significant. Partnership and participation demonstrates the importance of creating new awareness among people in poverty, and this has consequences for how we intervene. Comparing different approaches through European co-operation counteracts the tendency to 'homogenize' problems, seeing them as universally the same, instead of recognizing particular needs where the groups, regions or countries affected do not have the power to express their special interests. Professionals have been shown to have the capacity to reformulate or create policy through projects. This shows how systematic knowledge and practice in local policy contexts can have broader impact. Legitimacy based on scientific knowledge is no longer sufficient. Knowledge must be associated with joint participation, anchoring its legitimacy in the capacity to:

- explore new situations, understanding the connection between global and local issues;
- take into account objective and subjective understanding from knowledge about processes of intervention and from reflection influencing future interventions;
- respond effectively to the needs and experience of agencies, researchers and the population involved.

About 300 social workers are playing a part in anti-poverty programmes.

Education

Social work has become involved in formal education in state schools, where reforms to achieve greater access, extend compulsory education by two years and develop complementary school welfare programmes (*acção social escolar*) are associated with Veiga Simão reform carried out in 1971. Welfare measures seek to combat high drop-out and failure rates, to create conditions for educational success and to compensate for educational disadvantage due to weak general welfare provision and socio-economic insecurity among people with poor standards of living. The Institute of Social Support at School and its agencies form the base for social workers' involvement.

Early activity in this field was limited to casework supporting pupils with difficulties at school, and their families, with mainly practical help. After 1974, the general social movement towards a welfare state included education and social work intervention in this field. It involves about a hundred social workers. New developments have included:

- reorganizing services to reach a wider population and range of problems;
- linking public agencies with local groups and associations to organize collective responses to problems of school transport, much-needed facilities and equipment, school meals and healthcare, free time and holiday camps, and school exchanges;
- collaboration with centres of pedagogic medicine to study educational failure, and various initiatives ranging from individual support to collective information and action projects to improve levels of educational success.

Towards the end of the 1970s, restrictive economic policies, particularly from the World Bank, redirected educational policies towards contributing to economic development (Stoer, 1986). As a result, social work intervention became directed towards supporting school administration on slim resources. Eventually, social work help was dispensed with in favour of intervention co-ordinated by other professionals, especially redundant teachers. Social action in schools as part of national education provision is now mainly concerned with managing and delivering benefits such as transport, food and school materials, where social needs emerge. Social work activity is residual, mainly concerned with individual cases where educational failure seems to stem from social and economic needs, and with occasional counselling to support school objectives. The residual nature of social action in education has accompanied the transfer of responsibility for it to local authorities. In this context, possibilities for social work involvement have increased.

Educational reform in the 1980s, stimulated by preparation for and membership of the European Union, and related policies of economic and social modernization, led to the transfer of educational initiatives to the local authorities. Thus a 'simultaneous crisis and consolidation of mass education in Portugal' (Stoer, 1994) created a move to use education as a tool for social empowerment, involving social work as part of this. The 'consolidation of formal schooling' was carried out 'through the measures which seek to ensure a wider and more continuous presence of Portuguese young people in school' (Stoer, 1986). These measures were supported by special programmes, predominantly the Interministerial Programme for the Promotion of Educational Success (PIPSE) and the Education for All Programme (PEPT).

PIPSE was created in 1987 for a three-year period, later increased to five. It sought to strengthen educational action and resources, reduce failure and increase the quality of education (Garcia, 1995) through projects to raise awareness of the need to mobilize actions to gain resources for 'emergency' areas designated on the basis of educational indicators and general socio-economic levels. Centrally-designed initiatives were implemented by multi-disciplinary local teams including social workers. Evaluation suggests that central management and progressive limitation of resources reduced teams to working on only peripheral approaches with limited results and variable assimilation into local practice (Garcia, 1995). PEPT, which began in the early 1990s, although wider in scope, is based on similar objectives. It develops projects in priority areas with higher rates of educational failure and drop-out. It is more decentralized, is established regionally, and links with local development initiatives. Social workers are involved in local projects, either directly as part of the teams of experts for education, or seconded from partnership agencies at local level. The crisis of official mass education which, as suggested above, is occurring at the same time as its consolidation, has generated since 1989 a new model of educational management. The principles of autonomy, decentralization and participation value schools as places where participative intervention involving the local community can take place.

PIPSE's final two years (1990–92) likewise stressed intervention centred on the school, working on problems arising from school issues rather than following national policies. Local projects supported by pedagogic support teams (NAPs) sought to mobilize educators and local communities to debate and act on educational problems in initiatives centred on schools. The same package of policy measures included the creation of vocational schools, designed to strengthen the links between education and labour market requirements: 'The aim is to restructure the relationship between education and a changing labour market, strengthening the role of the school in the Portuguese modernisation process' (Stoer, 1994).

This change in education policy offers potential for social work involvement. The reforms of the 1980s have strengthened two new areas of intervention:

- under the Psychology and Guidance Services (SPOs), 'specialized educational support units' integrated into schools (Law 1990/91) aim to support pupils, provide complementary activities and promote school–community links. It is planned to integrate social workers into these teams;
- links between local development and school initiatives have generated special social projects.

Academic training has given priority to these fields, allowing alternative perspectives to traditional individual practice in schools to develop. ISSS Oporto, for example, offers a degree course linking modules on the Theory and Practice of Social Intervention, and a Seminar on Research into Social Service and Probation. Student placements in school projects focus on social and educational processes in schools, mobilizing and mediating between educational agencies and local agencies interested in promoting education. The main subject areas are as follows:

- school, family and community links, aiming at closer relationships between school and local agencies;
- work with co-ordinators and heads of classes, seeking to stimulate interaction between educational agencies, and to intervene in 'class and pupil problems';
- surveys on educational failure and dropping-out, and new school or local problems affecting education;
- collaboration in projects and activities to complement the curriculum, to support pupils with special needs, and extra-curricular activities;
- strengthening representative mechanisms for students' and parents' interests.

Despite education's importance, it involves only about fifty social workers in the whole country, but greater contributions from social work are possible and should be achieved in the future, by linking the development of general welfare provision with a broader role for local authorities in education.

Local authorities and local action

In this area, we will consider not only the history and current configuration of local authority powers, but also the emergence and development of other local activity (more or less formally organized) in the areas of recreational and cultural action, and local projects with a community dimension.

Before 1974, the state gave priority to the economy. Social affairs were delegated to the Catholic Church, which was the link between the state and civil society. For decades, local authorities were almost exclusively responsible for the infrastructure, tax collection and policing. Except for basic social assistance, social and economic policy and local development was outside the scope of local authorities. A major effect of the political changes of April 1974 was the strengthening of local power and the capacity to act on local social objectives. 'The written constitution (1976), in assigning to local authorities the pursuit of the interests of their respective populations, enshrined intervention in social policy issues as a local authority power' (Branco, 1991). The serious housing shortage, especially social housing, and the lack of social facilities, were the first great areas of local authority investment, and social workers became involved because of the social nature of these priorities.

Laws on local authority responsibilities and finances (later amended after pressure from the newly-established National Association of Portuguese Local Authorities) were enacted in 1977 and 1978 respectively. Later legislation progressively extended local authority responsibilities, but failure to allocate resources 'leads to the conclusion that the local authorities do not have significant responsibilities in the area of social policy' (Branco, 1991). Legal responsibilities for teaching and education from 1977, health and the protection of children and elderly people from 1984, and management of housing stock and related facilities mean that the 'principal areas of interest and the principal vocation of the local authorities are frequently, not to say predominantly, seen both by themselves and by others as centred essentially on the social as opposed to economic' (Cardoso, 1990).

More recently, local authorities have become involved in local development, challenging centralization, but also practising 'local development ... as the locality of "another" development' (Henriques, 1990a). This view of local development has emerged from local community interests and takes a different view of development from the central priority given to economics: 'the existence of a *"project of hope"* as a point of reference for individual and collective action, a *process of defence and mobilization of resources* with a view to the satisfaction of the basic needs of local communities and *the mobilization of active solidarity for the reconstruction of socio-community life*' (Henriques, 1990a). Geographical diversity and strong local traditions have led to a multiplicity of innovative initiatives for promoting local development. The attempt to link local to global and European trends is one of the most innovative aspects of this trend.

Henriques (1990b) identifies the most important aspects of local authority intervention as mobilizing local communities for development, reducing problems in meeting basic needs, concern for a sustainable environment, mobilizing local economic activity, mobilizing the 'independent' sector, implementing regional and urban planning, and strengthening local power through co-operation with other levels of authority. While such a range of achievements is not demonstrated everywhere, this finding shows the social development potential of local authorities. The success of local initiatives and failings in central direction of welfare activities have led to reassessment of the possibilities of all sorts of decentralization. Examples are local groups concerned with social, recreational, sporting and cultural activities, and formal initiatives like local development agencies, integrated community intervention projects, and increased acknowledgement of the importance of local identity and culture. In Portuguese tradition, recreational, cultural and sporting groups have played more of a role in communities than their obvious activities imply. The structure of such associations is almost always a close and sociable network of fairly restricted groups of residents, and they have assumed diversified roles in everyday life, such as:

- organizing and developing areas and activities for leisure, social contacts and recreation not covered by official organizations;
- serving as training grounds for social integration activities, and promoting public participation;
- providing opportunities for sharing and mutual support in dealing with local problems;
- acting as a local 'citizens' reserve', prepared to be involved in other issues.

These associations are rooted in volunteering and local initiatives, and maintain a precarious equilibrium between independence and dependence on public support (Rodrigues and Stoer, 1993). Because they have recently succeeded in contributing substantially to some communities, they have received greater attention from local authorities.

Since local authorities and organizations are clearly dependent on central and global trends for the success of their efforts and central, European and global initiatives depend on local action for success, economic and social development increasingly comes to require incorporation of every level. Thus local action shapes how central initiatives operate, and counteracts centralizing tendencies. Social work has managerial functions in local social projects as well as involvement in promoting local development. Therefore, the shift in emphasis to local power makes local action a promising field for the future of social work in Portugal. This is transforming traditional fields of action, for example in the assessment and analysis role in local slum clearance and rehousing projects. Debate about as yet unfulfilled decentralization continues to influence professional action.

Social workers' roles in local authority and community development and action have brought numerous benefits: 'greater proximity to problems and identification of needs ... more direct identification and mobilization of existing capacity and potential ... opportunities for reflection and inter-disciplinary practice and integrated intervention ... challenge to inter-agency co-operation ... laboratory of experiences and innovative solutions ... integration of quantitative and qualitative dimensions of development ... adoption of new, more decentralized mechanisms of regulation of local conflicts and contradictions ... trying out new forms of economic and social operation – "partnership economy" and "welfare society", alternatives to the traditional state–market dichotomy ... challenge to the central and local state to emerge as an indispensable partner and not as a mere "tax authority" and "controller of these processes" ' (Amaro, 1994).

By being involved with local authorities and local action, social work is not limited to service delivery, but can respond to social issues holistically. Close knowledge of the population and local organizations' problems and needs offers more diverse roles. Social work took on the role of mediator in promoting local development, and this provides a new arena for social work interventions.

Training in this area combines understanding of local interactions and intervention and analysis in particular fields: services where social work has a longer tradition of involvement, such as housing and social facilities, those which have emerged more recently, such as the environment, developing local organizations and cultural action and integrated local development projects, specialist projects, and studies and surveys linked to programmes planning and intervention. About 5 per cent of the 4,000 or so 'parishes' (the smallest unit of secular local government) and 50 per cent of the 350 town councils already make use of social workers in this role. Polysocial is a social workers' association working in this field to share experience, provide information, debate, disseminate ideas and provide training. Two early seminars have taken place on local authorities and social work, and local authorities and decentralization.

Social work education

Social work education started in the 1930s. The first colleges were in Lisbon (1935) and Coimbra (1937), under the legal framework of the Ministry of Education. These were private colleges, supported by Catholic organizations. In 1956, the organization of courses and programmes was reformulated, and the Oporto college was created with the same legal status. Education in private colleges reflected the ambiguous academic status of social work. The training, organized over four years, had the same access and curriculum structure as state university education, and it became a recognized higher education course in 1961. However, no academic degree was conferred – a power then restricted to the state university. The lack of academic and professional status led to discontent and campaigning by colleges and professionals. After 1974, with democratization and trends towards a welfare state under way, clarifying social work's academic status by integrating the colleges into state education was considered. The colleges steadily disconnected themselves academically and institutionally from Catholic support bodies, and re-organized themselves to conform with the model of state education, while the state became responsible for all their funding. This trend was reversed with liberalization policies in the 1980s. Preparation for membership of the EC, and growing devaluation of social and welfare state policies, made their integration into state universities (which were also suffering a decline in funding) politically untenable.

Subsequently, however, private and co-operative higher education was regulated, starting in 1985 and completed in 1989, because of its important contribution to higher education, in particular the political significance of greater access to higher education. The new legal framework allowed for formal recognition as an academic degree for a course then organized over five years, and granted university status to the colleges. They were integrated into the national education system, through diplomas, in September 1989.

The social and political changes of 1974 created conditions for new developments in theory and method. The most important developments were the secularization of curricula, the repositioning of social work as a social science, and the political commitment to ongoing democratization in society. The 1970s and 1980s saw the following trends in the curricula:

- theory courses were geared towards understanding structural approaches to social problems, particularly using concepts from economics, sociology and law;
- theoretical and practical aspects of different disciplines were focused on a combination of analysis and intervention;
- the policy context of social work was expressed as a more explicit commitment to establishing general and specific rights.

Further developments came about within the new regulations for private higher education with the aim of justifying recognition of the academic degree. Colleges have their own specializations, but basic trends are:

- developing capacities for analysis and conceptualization in understanding social problems in their social context;
- updating and consolidating understanding and practice preparation for carrying out varied tasks within both well-established professional roles and within emerging roles derived from the European context;
- strengthening theoretical and practical training in research, and extending knowledge, with a particular focus on Portuguese situations.

These curricula aim to provide future professionals with broad skills for intervention, together with a capacity to analyse and conceptualize new forms of practice. Students should develop thoughtful and critical analyses of social issues, and examine practical approaches to problems, organizations and a range of fields of action (Rodrigues, 1990). Linking theory with practice offers a model of social work method which brings knowledge and forward-looking intervention together with social change. At ISSS Oporto, for example, fieldwork placements during the last two years of the course bring together intervention and research, through courses on the theory and practice of social intervention and seminars on social work research.

There is a clear correlation between the recognition of new fields of professional involvement and areas of research and action studied in qualifying education. Innovative political and agency initiatives also contribute to service developments. We hope this will lead to a long-lasting interchange between professional activity and training, nourished by other initiatives discussed below.

New demands on social work beyond long-standing areas of action, new and old problems and new ways of dealing with them, have led to academic and professional investment, namely post-graduate education research and continuing post-qualifying training.

Lisbon and Oporto Colleges have developed a post-graduate programme, initially offering a qualification for teaching and research in social work. Ministry recognition of the teaching qualification is not practicable, and it is being developed with the Catholic University of São Paolo, Brazil. Three courses leading to teaching qualifications were completed between 1987 and 1995, two in social work (ISSS Lisbon) and one in social work and social policy (ISSS Oporto). Already over forty professionals and teachers are academically qualified, and useful research and professional outcomes contribute to meeting the need for analytical material in the field of social work (see the bibliography for some helpful examples demonstrating the value and diversity of the materials becoming available).

Government decrees of March 1995 empowered the colleges to confer the degree of Master of Social Work and Social Policy (ISSS Oporto) and Social Work (ISSS Lisbon) in their own right. This landmark move should strengthen training through developing systematic study and research, drawing in several academic disciplines and increasing teacher training in social work. We need to invest in following up recognition of these qualifications, expanding beyond academic training to specialized post-graduate courses led by working professionals. This should contribute to reshaping training to meet the new social and agency requirements. Among the initiatives are courses in social management (ISSS Lisbon) and psychosocial intervention in health (ISSS Oporto). A 1994 seminar on intervention through research presented results from post-graduate training with the aim of debating progress, 'not only in technical skills and know-how, but in structural and interdisciplinary understanding of social issues and change understood and elaborated in direction, objectives and strategies of professional action' (ISSSL 1994). Other recent academic developments include:

- study and research centres linked to the educational institutions at Oporto, Lisbon and Coimbra, with research, debate and dissemination objectives;
- the Portuguese Centre for Research into Social History and Social Work, based in Lisbon;
- the Association for Research and Debate on Social Work, based in Oporto, pursuing, among other aims, information, debate, studies and research on professional practice.

Two regular journals containing information on practice experience, features and opinion are published: *Intervenção Social* by Lisbon ISSS, and *Do Serviço Social* by the Association of Social Service Professionals (APSS). Information about these is contained in the bibliography.

The growing complexity, development and reshaping of the social domain, the need to disseminate new findings, and the importance given to the best use of human resources have led to efforts to provide continuing education and in-service training. This is promoted by professional, research and academic organizations, supported by the social work colleges. Initiatives have recently been organized around the following subjects:

- macro-social subjects such as the state and social policy;
- the fields of intervention, intervention and research methods, and practice processes and procedures;
- developing social work agencies;
- approaches to new subjects and debates to familiarize colleagues with potential fields of practice.

Diverse subjects have been covered, with a wide range of participants, and considerable time is devoted to such continuing education efforts. The time devoted to debate and informal discussion is an important aspect of such training. It also stimulates links between professional practice and academic fields, benefiting both, and supports the recognition of fields of study and practice which are as yet not well accepted.

Endword: Themes and issues in Portuguese policy and social work

Social work has become important in Portugal among the social disciplines and professions. The welfare state may be fragile, but this means that social problems are not fragmented among many different professions, co-operation between professionals is enhanced, and roles exist for many different professional groups, even those, like social work, which have emerged recently. It also means that innovative practice and diverse activities are more possible than in a well-established, structured pattern of services. 'Fire-fighting' with conventional approaches co-exists with more thoughtful practice, taking into account a variety of influences and interests.

The original foundation of social work in the social doctrine of the Church may have counterbalanced practice solely based on assumed individual causes of problems. This left the way open for greater awareness and flexibility in using analysis and intervention in the face of social change.

The broad issues affecting social work in Portugal recently are:

- a focus on consolidating democratization, emphasizing the participation of a variety of professionals, agencies and specialisms;
- a move away from practice centred on individuals, to include both local and central structural influences;
- a more pluralist approach to theory and method, in line with the diversity of activity;
- the use of more specialized approaches and extensive knowledge, alongside better skills training, thus combining knowledge and action more effectively.

The main direction of development in the role of social workers is as follows:

- direct provision of practical help, follow-up and guidance in problem situations, giving prominence to individualized psychosocial assessment and support, support for rehabilitation into society and employment for disabled people, psychosocial support and social re-integration for, for example, unemployed people, ex-prisoners and drug users;

- projects in response to social needs, such as collective facilities, action to improve housing conditions, infrastructure and outdoor spaces, school health projects and preventing educational failure and drop-out;

- study and planning – socio-economic and cultural studies of districts and communities, social studies of urban districts aimed at integrating marginalized communities, study and evaluation of working conditions to counter accidents at work and absenteeism, and studies of the needs of particular group situations and at-risk populations;

- basic education, training and sociocultural activism or enlivenment – cultural work, training for young people, health education (for example, nutrition and family planning), public awareness of the problems of at-risk groups, and information on social resources and rights;

- social organization and participation – support for creating and mobilizing, for example, residents' groups, cultural associations, youth groups.

Social workers act directly, and also undertake co-ordination and administration, and work in assessment and consultancy, research and education. All this is taking place in a context of applying theory to practice, and new efforts to strengthen learning and achieve interdisciplinary understanding.

8 Social work in Spain

Teresa Rossell and Josefina Fernández

Introduction

Social work is still a young profession in Spain, developing later than in most Western European countries. Its main period of growth took place when democracy was re-established and a modern legal framework allowed the advancement of social services and the resources to support them. Two different political systems provided the backcloth to social work's origins: Franco's dictatorship (1939–75), and the democracy established on the basis of the Spanish Constitution in 1978. Each system had a different conception of the state and of law, and consequently, a different point of view about social problems and needs and how we should respond to them. Therefore, changing political, legal and social policy contexts have influenced the evolution of social work. At the same time, social workers' expertise and commitment, abilities and dreams have contributed to the shaping of social work's present identity.

To understand and assess social work in Spain requires a brief consideration of its historical path, its principal current influences, the conjunction of different factors in its evolution, and an outline of future trends. Within this framework, we focus on three fields: social services for children and young people, the care of young offenders and social work in the mental health services. Finally, we give a brief account of social work education.

The context of social work in Spain

Social work under the dictatorship

Despite economic growth in the twentieth century, the legal and social protection systems and the organizational development of social services did not

117

allow social work to develop fully until the 1970s. Social action was still derived from the Law of Beneficence of 1849, and care for children, families, the elderly and mentally ill people had to be organized under its provisions.

The lead in the modern development of social work from the late 1950s was taken mainly by the Roman Catholic Church and quasi-state bodies. Social workers started working in places like hospitals, residential homes or parishes. Here, their aims and functions were poorly understood, but were enlisted to the aims of various organizations in responding to equally ill-defined social problems.

At the beginning, social workers had part-time contracts or were asked to join the complement of staff in other services, such as holiday camps, the first social services for handicapped people, started by voluntary organizations (e.g. ASPANIAS, ECOM, AUXILIA). Those first roles led to the creation of the first units, or departments, of social work. These grew up first on the personal initiative of hospital, residential home or parish directors, and not as a part of a general development plan. Among the first social workers, who were very few in number until the end of the dictatorship, were professionals with a very good training from social work schools which had offered specialized training in various fields, and were highly-motivated staff with great creative capacities. Their pioneering work meant that professional functions and systematic methods in social intervention came to be recognized. They made significant contributions to reducing the rigidity of care given to clients as social care institutions began to change.

During those years, social workers helped to establish the first associations for people with psychological, physical and sensory disabilities. They helped create occupational workshops for chronically sick or disabled people, associations for families of mentally ill people, and opened the first recreational centres for the elderly and handicapped people. Despite the problems around them, social workers of the 1960s developed their professional skills through international contacts, supervision and their own creative spirit. They became experts on health, education, mental health and children, among other social work fields.

In 1968, a Catholic Church organization, Diocesan Caritas, started 'community social work centres' in some parishes across the country, where social workers initiated a new form of social work practice. The main characteristic was to develop people's consciousness of and sensitivity towards their own problems, lack of care provision and services, and to enhance their participation in responding to them. Social workers worked with groups of marginalized people living on the outskirts of major cities lacking sufficient infrastructure, and helped them to set up hygiene, transport, schooling, social and sport services. They worked mainly among immigrants from other parts of Spain (Gypsies) concerned with both their own ethnic identity and problems of integration within wider communities. At that time, social workers helped underground political groups and encouraged neighbour-hood associations which played an important role in achieving political change. Community work offered experience of a new professional method, a critical attitude in social work, and spurred ideas of integrating different forms of professional practice. It developed community practice that encouraged joint action with the community in order to create new resources and services that had not existed before and which were managed by their users. Also, they helped to create different types of associations and re-establish social and political rights. This practice was more fully conceptualized later, significantly influencing later Spanish ideas supporting the inclusion of a community perspective in social work practice.

The critical attitude shown by social workers in the late 1960s was not exclusive to community workers, but was also shared by other social workers, who were very critical of social institutions, following Bassaglia's ideas. They reflected upon and denounced the high power of professionals like doctors, lawyers and even social workers themselves. Other factors contributed to the formation of this critical trend among progressive professionals and students. Among these were the extended end of the dictatorship, and the unknown political future of the country, the Paris troubles of May 1968 (which had a considerable impact in Spain), the growth of critical ideology towards institutions, and the anti-psychiatry movement.

Another critical trend of the 1970s which had a strong influence on Spanish social work was the 'reconceptualization' movement in Latin America. Among its influences were proposals to make political and ideological allegiances with clients, and to integrate methods to avoid divisive interventions carried out according to service specialities, geographical divisions or the ages of clients. From these contributions came the idea of gathering traditional social work methods into what was called the 'basic method' (Colomer, 1974). This proposes the same social work intervention process being focused, without losing a perception of the whole, on different levels of care: personal, family, group or community.

Although the radical idealism of some professionals was sometimes unrealistic, all these changes had a very positive effect on social work's progress. In the last years of Franco's dictatorship and during the period of transition into democracy from 1972 to 1987, social work gained recognition as a profession that had elaborated a model of practice which contained different methods and levels of intervention, which mainly supported leftist ideologies, and which sought a model of social welfare policy where social care and services were to be mainly a public responsibility.

Models and proposals during the transition period

During the transition years between dictatorship and democracy, social workers influenced the development of three models or trends in the planning of new social services networks. Although separable analytically, all three models have been treated as compatible and complementary.

The main trend sought the establishment in Spain of the European welfare model, based on exclusively public responsibility for services and a system of social protection that should meet the needs of all citizens. The emphasis here was to promote social laws, services and resources which did not exist at the time. In this model, social workers were to serve as dispensers of services, linking needs and resources (Heras and Cortajarena, 1979). This approach was encouraged by the Socialist Party from the Dirección General de Asuntos Sociales. Despite the decentralized model of the state defined by the Spanish Constitution, the Dirección General de Asuntos Sociales created the *Plan Concertado*, which set the general lines of a policy for social action and social work. Some regional authorities have pursued this enthusiastically, as they did not have their own model. The plan requires local authorities to share responsibility by financing 50 per cent of projects, but also stimulated local authorities to establish projects which could not have been set up without their intervention.

A second model, also pursuing a welfare state, emphasized how local social services could co-ordinate service and resource provision while promoting citizen responsibility and participation. Barcelona's local authority provides a good example. It was considered 'the model' of local social services during the first years of the Spanish democracy (Doménech, 1989). Basic principles were universalization, normalization, decentralization and sectorization, trying, as with education and health services, to reduce the perception of social services as 'poor services for poor people'. These principles became the basic concepts underlying the regional governments' social services laws.

A third trend emphasized ideological, theoretical and professional aspects rather than organization. It was therefore complementary rather than in opposition to the 'official' discourse (Rossell, 1987). This approach was known, first in Catalonia and then in Euskadi and Andalusia, as the 'health' or 'clinical' model. It promotes a professional social work concern with clients' human worth, and promotes personal autonomy and social workers' solidarity as professionals. Although workers best achieve their ends as part of agencies, they are not blindly subordinate to agency policies. They are professionals who promote the growth of natural networks, self-help organizations, and preserve natural bonding, and who need a thorough and meticulous training in their functions and activities.

Democracy and the Constitution

In 1978, the Spanish Constitution was approved, making Spain an *estado de derecho* (state of law). As with the idea of the 'rule of law', official bodies are limited in the possible arbitrary use of power, and the state's functions are based on citizens' possession of inherent, inviolable human rights. The idea of democracy brings with it the idea of citizen participation in decisions which may affect them. An innovative aspect of the Constitution was the inclusion of the unique concept of the 'social state'. Thus, access to social services is clearly established as every citizen's right. Human dignity and freedom requires the state to be responsible for providing positive social benefits that make the exercise of freedom possible, so the Constitution establishes citizen participation in political, economical, cultural and social life.

Promoting participation is a complete U-turn from the previous situation. It provides a framework for practising true social community work whose aim is citizens' participation in developing their communities. People should be enabled to become active and contribute to their country's history as active and responsible subjects. The legal framework of the Constitution gives support to social work and social policy in the following provisions:

- Trade unions and business associations are recognized as defenders of their own social and economic interests (article 7).
- The right of association is recognized (article 22).
- Workers have the rights to strike and participate in collective wage negotiation (articles 28–37).
- Public social security has been established (article 41).
- Associations of clients and consumers are promoted (article 51).
- Professional associations and organizations are acknowledged (articles 36–52).
- Regulations for the participation of organizations and associations in decision-making processes on matters which affect them have been enacted (article 105).
- Rules and regulations govern co-operative industries (article 129).
- Trade unions and other associations may take part in planning general economic activity (article 131).

The Spanish Constitution proclaims solidarity among the nationalities and regions, and also guarantees economic equilibrium among regions, where there is diversity of language, culture and different degrees of economic development. The solidarity principle is applied to the 17 autonomous communities, which each have a government and parliament with rights to legislate on matters within their competence. One of these is to plan, organize and manage social services. Each autonomous community must legislate on social services. However, social services are a local responsibility under the 1985 Reform of Local Authorities Act (*Ley de Régimen Local*). All municipalities with more than 20,000 inhabitants organize their own social services;

towns with lower populations are supported by other local government bodies, like the *diputaciones*.

In Catalonia, the administrative divisions are:

- towns and municipalities;
- *comarca* (county);
- *diputación* (province);
- *comunidad autónoma* (regional government);
- *estado* (the state).

Services developed with citizens' help and participation belong, generally, to municipalities and townships. Where they are more complex, sophisticated or expensive, needing more complex organization, the 'autonomous community' is responsible.

The new organization of public services strongly influenced the evolution of social work. After local authority elections, local ('primary care') social services were created. The politicians responsible for establishing them were unfamiliar with what was required. However, the expanded job market led to full employment for social workers, and for many, it was their first post, so they started their practice creating new services in contexts where they had not existed before.

During their early years, these new services had to face the consequences of economic difficulties caused by the 'oil crisis' of the 1970s. This led to many demands for material help. In some cases, experienced social workers managed to create job-creation projects for young people and projects involving better-off areas of towns to promote employment. Elsewhere, new services and social workers needed more time to get organized and offer projects to the population. In some cases, this became the origin of bureaucratic attitudes which regarded social workers as dispensers of resources, creating frustration and unbalancing their professional role. Other professionals, such as psychologists and educationalists, came into social services and were a source of insecurity to social workers, who came to accept claims on their professional functions from these new professionals.

Home care services, organized and managed by local social services, and a growing number of voluntary organizations have been important resources for care.

The role of voluntary organizations and the Roman Catholic Church

The Spanish Constitution established the right of association, provided organizations have legal status, except for secret and paramilitary associations.

The basic law on association originates from pre-democratic times (1964), but requires internal organization to be on democratic lines. A new law, more in tune with the current situation, is needed. 'Youth organizations', where members are between 14 and 30 years of age, are regulated within the constitutional framework by a special decree of 1988. Catalonia has an exceptional number and range of voluntary associations, which have contributed to knowledge of needs in the region and maintaining traditions that might disappear without their social initiatives.

The Catalan Social Services Law promotes voluntary movements. Social initiatives have been acknowledged, and public authorities are required to promote citizen participation in planning and controlling social services. The importance of voluntary action is also recognized, and non-profitmaking private initiatives in social services are regulated. According to a study by the Catalan Government (Generalitat de Catalunya, 1985) there were 23,711 associations, 277 private foundations and 4,500 co-operative societies. These numbers are increasing yearly.

We have previously noted the role of the Catholic Church in social care. During the dictatorship, the few inadequate educational, health, justice and social public services were provided for specific groups, such as sick people, children, young people, the elderly or offenders. The few community services and recreational centres for elderly people were for specific kinds of people. There were no services for families, except those specifically aimed at poor people. The only primary care services were the medical services offered by social security services, which had important failings. Little attention was given to prevention. As a result, people avoided public services as soon as they had enough income for private services. Private schools were mainly run by religious orders, and were influential. Religious orders were generally present in hospitals, residential homes and asylums, even though they were administered by local government. Also, Caritas operated in parishes. Consequently, the Catholic Church was, almost exclusively, the agent of social, educational, health and recreational services. The progressive wing of the Catholic Church had a major role under the dictatorship in preserving culture, promoting liberal and anti-fascist ideals and actively resisting Franco's rule. However, the pre-eminence of Church welfare services and the Church's official links with the political regime created a strong negative reaction towards Church institutions in spite of some of their progressive elements.

In the early years, municipal local services were therefore in conflict with existing services. Public services provision was idealized, and it was generally felt that lay and leftist groups were the exclusive source of good ideas. There were negative and stereotyped reactions to other contributions. Time resolved many of these conflicts. Relations with public social services, and those provided by other agencies such as Red Cross and local associations, became more harmonious as they became adapted to new laws, and as new services matured. Voluntary organizations made significant innovations in approaching new social problems, and in turn have achieved general recognition.

In spite of early adverse reactions, once public authority was established, it could acknowledge the important role of non-public organizations in the welfare of those population groups which were outside the care and control role of public services. Public authorities and voluntary organizations started co-operating covertly, until new European trends proclaiming the 'failure' of the welfare state opened the way to partnership and 'coming back to the people'. With this came support and recognition of voluntary organizations and their inclusion in the planning and management of social provision.

Social work practice

Social work practice in the early 1990s

In 1990, the idea of a welfare state and of public social services as the only provision was abandoned. Although the political will exists to achieve this, co-operation with non-governmental organizations is sought. Neither minimum income benefit nor employment programmes have relieved unemployment and growing poverty among some parts of the population. Universal provision of social services seems difficult during a recession. Strictly economic needs have taken priority over other benefits. There is also a growth in the number of migrants, domestic violence, physical and sexual abuse (which are seen as new phenomena in Spain, where abuse has been traditionally linked to alcoholism), and new poor and urban groups such as skinheads and neo-fascists. Unemployment among social workers is growing. Students experience difficulty in finding a post on graduation. Local government has, with few exceptions, reduced social expenditure and, consequently, there are fewer job opportunities for social workers.

Social services focus on clients' basic needs. Sometimes, the social services are unable to resolve problems which are structural and derive from international trends. Some writers argue that this creates unease and a negative self-perception among social workers as they take the role of 'managers of poverty' (Ubieto, 1994). Social workers experience pressure from both their agencies and clients, especially those working in primary care. Their stress, loneliness and complaints are not reflected in research or theory. None the less, there are new opportunities and initiatives in unemployment and self-help projects involving volunteers which offer a more stimulating outlook.

Social services for children and young people

In the past, child care was undertaken by charities. 'Charity houses' caring for children were managed by local organizations (*diputaciones*), and also provided for elderly people. The institutions cared for deserted or illegitimate children, and also fostered those whose families had no means to raise them. Parallel to the *diputaciones*, there were the Obra de Protección de Menores (Child Protection Agency), which developed as a result of a consolidated law of 1948, and the Tribunales Tutelares de Menores (Courts for the Guardianship of Children and Young People), which protected neglected children and dealt with young offenders.

Diputaciones, councils for the protection of children, Tribunales Tutelares de Menores and residential homes in big cities were the earliest employers of social workers in the child care field. They worked with families and prepared them to adopt children. The first adoption services were organized within the *diputaciones*, since they managed residential homes for pregnant women who wanted to have their children adopted.

Children's services were mainly large residential homes, and offered the opportunity to undertake only very basic social work. The characteristics of the provision were:

● There were no admission criteria or social histories. Children were admitted according to the urgency of their case and their position on a waiting list.
● The period of residence was unlimited, usually until children reached adulthood.
● No work was done with their families, who were also not involved in their children's education.
● Homes were large and isolated from the outside world.
● Schooling was inside the home, and the same people cared for the children during school and 'home' time (*Diputació de Barcelona*, 1987).

From 1981 to 1982, during the first democratic period, there were reforms in residential homes and in general children's services. The new approach was as follows:

● Children and young people were to be cared for as near as possible to their own environment. Placing them in residential homes and separating them from their families was to be avoided as far as possible.
● Homes were turned into small living units, such as family homes or small residential homes.
● A personal working plan was to be developed with each child and their family. They were approached by a multi-disciplinary team consisting

of a social worker, a pedagogue and a psychologist. In some cases, a medical doctor and a lawyer were brought in.

● Alternative measures, such as foster families and adoption, were promoted (Generalitat de Catalunya, 1985).

In 1987, a major legal change took place with the reform of the Civil Code on Adoption Matters. Despite its title, this also meant a change in general care provision for children. This law originated the concept of 'defenceless' as a notion of 'the state a child finds himself in when he does not receive adequate care from his parents or other people legally in charge of him'. Also, for the first time, judges could not permit a child's adoption without a proposal from the public authority for that child. Children must remain with their families as much as possible, and if children must be separated from them, they must be reunited as soon as possible. Foster care was regulated, almost for the first time since it had been established by decree during the Second Republic but not implemented during the period of Franco's rule. Autonomous regional governments were to be the competent public authorities to implement this law. They had to carry out the requirements using professional staff, mainly social workers, but psychologists, pedagogues and lawyers were also involved.

The new law reduced legal jurisdiction within social services for children. Judges were compelled to ask for social work or other professional assessments when placing children for adoption or fostering without the consent of the family of origin. Although this was partly a response to social workers seeking more autonomy and a higher regard for their role, the law provoked an ambivalent reaction. The changes brought social workers great satisfaction, but they meant greater responsibility for social workers in making sometimes difficult decisions in child protection issues, proposing 'defenceless' status and in assessing adoption cases or foster homes.

Central government, through its Child Study Centre, organized training courses and seminars for social workers from all over the country. The initial anxiety about carrying new responsibilities vanished as they felt more secure and better trained. The social work role in this field is well-established, and proposals for further development are arising from experience and practice. Work in this field includes both direct work with the family, children or other people important to the children's care, and indirect work involving institutions, organizations or children's own home communities.

Care for young offenders

The 1987 change in child care law also modified the old law of the Guardianship Courts in child protection. However, the criminal role of the courts remained unchanged, even though some legal provisions were clearly unconstitutional, as was confirmed in 1991 by a ruling of the Constitutional Court. The law was clearly paternalist, and did not offer young offenders legal guarantees of protection. There was no age limit: children of any age could be prosecuted if they were alleged to have broken the law. Also, there was no time limit to some of the sanctions which could be applied, mainly warnings, surveillance and custody. The need for a juvenile criminal law is clear, but it has not been promulgated so far. To respond to the Constitutional Court ruling, an organic law was promulgated in June 1992, reforming the unconstitutional law and procedures of juvenile courts. This reform introduced a minimum age of 12 before prosecution can proceed. Adult status for criminal prosecution is attained at 18, according to the Criminal Code (1995) which has increased the age from 16. This new penal age, however, will not be applied until a new criminal law is promoted.

The reformed law also establishes children's rights to be defended by lawyers. Judges must maintain all the legal guarantees of ordinary trials. Provision has also been made for restitution to be made to the victim, and to provide community service as a sentence. These measures, which are common in other countries even for adults, did not previously exist in Spain, so this is a great step forward. It enhances personal responsibility among young people, which has educational benefits, as they make amends for their offences. Recognition of the need for similar sanctions in criminal law for adults is growing in public debate, and their development for young people may provide important evidence of their success.

Social workers are charged with organizing and supervising restitution measures for young offenders. In some cases, social workers must persuade the victim to co-operate, as there is little history of this approach to offending in Spain. For example, one social worker mentioned her difficulties in persuading the telephone company to accept restitution from two youngsters whose offence was to paint graffiti in telephone booths, but after they cleaned the booths, the company expressed satisfaction to them. To organize and supervise restitution in Catalonia, the Juvenile Justice Directorate has established a mediation service which has achieved excellent results so far and is having a great influence in creating a positive climate for 'mediation' in the general population (Departament de Justícia, 1992).

As in adoption procedures, the Juvenile Court Law requires a technical team to support judges. When a young person is found guilty, the team reports on the young person's psychological, educational, family and social circumstances. Social workers are generally responsible for these reports, analysing all social and family aspects and other circumstances that may have influenced criminal behaviour. A diagnostic assessment must be carried out with other team members when necessary.

Although not perfect, this last reform has been a great step forward in provision for young offenders, and has widened the opportunities for social work to practise successfully in implementing such measures as mediation. The social workers' role is also recognized, as their social reports on the young person must be considered by the judge, although following their recommendations is discretionary.

Social work in mental health

The involvement of social workers in mental health services has been out-standing, and has enabled a significant development of the profession. The third Spanish social work school started in 1953, promoted by a professor of psychiatry, Dr Sarró, and was located in the school of medicine, sharing the psychiatry department's premises. At that time, psychiatric care was mainly provided in asylums and was the legal responsibility of the local authority (*diputaciones*), governed by the Law of Beneficence, dating from the nine-teenth century. Mentally ill people were not considered ill, but poor and alienated, in need of welfare care rather than medical and healing attention. This situation meant that social workers starting work in psychiatric hospitals had to re-introduce mentally ill people to their home environment. They worked with patients' families, giving them support and counselling to facilitate patients' return home. This was a very difficult task in the context of patients being considered incurable and needing to be secluded from society.

In the 1970s, the anti-psychiatry movement, led mainly by Laing and Cooper in the United Kingdom, and Basaglia in Italy, had influence in Spain. Many social workers became strong supporters of this movement, as they thought it would lead to better understanding of mental illness, and they favoured caring for the sick in their own communities. At a less radical level, social workers identified themselves with the social psychiatry movement initially started by Maxwell Jones (1968). In Spain, both movements con-fronted methods that were totalitarian and non-participative. Because of this, some psychiatrists and social workers who followed the anti-psychiatric model were dismissed from their jobs in the Asturias Psychiatric Hospital and Conxo Psychiatric Hospital in Santiago de Compostela (Galicia).

In the mid-1970s, professional groups working in the field of mental health started mental health community centres with the aim of caring for mentally ill people in their own communities. These were private, non-profitmaking centres that had difficulty in surviving. Their aim was to be incorporated into the public services network.

In 1981, a group of social workers of Catalonia published an article in a professional review about the deplorable conditions of the mentally ill and their difficulties in achieving re-integration within their own communities (Aragonés et al., 1981). They argued that psychiatric care should be incor-porated in general health services, and asked for resources to rehabilitate mentally ill people in the community. In the same year, the Barcelona *diputación* started using a care model based on community psychiatry, and made the 'mental hygiene centres' join the public services network. They also promoted the creation of new primary care mental health centres covering all of Barcelona Province. The basic teams in these centres consisted of psychiatrists, psychologists and social workers. The network centres were primary care centres, day hospitals, psychiatric units in general hospitals and the already existing psychiatric hospitals.

This networking approach was progressively implemented in other areas as well, and led to widespread recognition of social workers in the mental health field. However, this was not easy, as many clinical professionals found it difficult to adopt the community practice model in daily practice. Social workers took, and are still taking, the responsibility for introducing a care model where social aspects of mental illness are taken into account within a wider perspective.

At present, mental healthcare is fully integrated into general health services. In Catalonia, the centres which formerly worked under the *diputaciones* are now contracted by the Institut Català de la Salut (ICS), the official Catalan institution for developing public health services.

There has been progress towards dealing with the criticisms of 1981, although there is still a lack of resources for rehabilitative facilities, such as day centres, supported housing and occupational workshops. A group of social workers reporting on the needs of their psychiatric patients for residential provision (Acosta et al., 1994) showed that 70 per cent of these patients would need some sort of residential home during their lives, and 28 per cent of them needed it already. Comparison of developing needs with existing resources suggests a requirement for supported housing and residential homes for seriously mentally ill people in the community. More provision in psychogeriatric and psychiatric hospitals is also needed for people who have no prospect of returning to their family or home environment. The focus of social work in mental health at present is to achieve progress towards meeting this need for more resources in the community.

Social work education

Spanish social work started in Barcelona from its first school, Escuela de Estudios Sociales para la Mujer, in 1934, inspired and guided by Belgian schools. After the Spanish Civil War (1936–39) and until 1957, there were only five social work schools in Spain, located in Madrid and Catalonia. There were only a few graduates, and they found jobs in industry, health and Church welfare services. During the 1960s, the number of social work schools grew, mainly from initiatives by the Roman Catholic Church, followed by other quasi-statutory bodies. Eventually, 42 social work schools were established across the country. Their existence is justified by economic growth, leading to a market for social work skills which could provide jobs for almost all graduates. In 1964, social work studies gained official academic recognition with a technical diploma.

In 1982, social work schools were integrated into the university system. They and their teachers thus became linked to an academic context that stimulates research and contacts with other subjects, and breaks down the influence of the Catholic Church on social work studies. It also means a wider understanding and acceptance of the profession. This and the growing job market led to increased enrolment of students. Schools have to cope with larger classes, which they have tried to balance by organizing seminars and practical training. Social work training lasts three years and leads to a diploma. Curricula can be more flexible than in the past, with optional subjects.

In 1993, with the implementation of the 1987 University Reform Act, all university curricula, including social work, were modified. Following the principles of decentralization and autonomy, all social work curricula consist of 50 per cent national curriculum and 50 per cent organized by each university according to its theoretical orientation and the social context it has to serve. Students are freer to choose their training, enhancing exchanges between departments and university divisions, and bringing a new vitality which stimulates the interest of lecturers and social workers.

Endword: Themes and issues in Spanish social work

Recent legislation on social issues has enabled the creation and consolidation of a network of services, programmes and resources that cater for many needs and problems. Some services are innovative and bring volunteers together in several sectors – public, private and voluntary – and encourage client participation. Social workers have made a significant contribution to the development of current social policy and services, sometimes through their direct responsibility in political and technical posts, sometimes through their practice with clients. Social workers have a leading role within various social services, although their status differs from one field to another according to the composition of multi-disciplinary teams.

Generally, the profession has made considerable progress. New theoretical and methodological approaches have been introduced. In particular, systems, ecological and socio-educational approaches have enriched and widened social work practice.

Partly because of developments in democracy and the growth of social services, new professions and para-professional workers have come into the social services field. Some of their tasks were formerly undertaken by social workers. This provoked confusion until functions and tasks were defined within teams. Current practice takes place within interdisciplinary teams with clear responsibilities and functions. In some, social workers co-ordinate the team; in others, social workers have lost pre-eminence in favour of psychologists and other professions with higher academic qualifications.

Another aspect of social work's evolution since the restoration of democracy has been the creation of an organization of public social services. In particular, primary care or local social services have achieved a strong identification of social work with social services for clients, both among social workers and the general public.

The effort and interest taken by social workers in establishing principles for organizing and implementing services, for allocating resources, and in developing data collection systems to analyse, diagnose and evaluate programmes led to an emphasis on these aspects and to less development of professional practice. Now that these aspects have been well established, social work seems to be gaining a new spirit, with greater assertiveness and a stronger self-identity. These can be observed through the social work journals *Revista de Trabajo Social*, published in Barcelona, and *Revista de Politica Social y Servicios Sociales*, published in Madrid. Social workers have increased the number and quality of their contributions, and communicate innovative professional experiences.

However, some aspects have still to be developed. To encourage the positive growth of social work in Spain, it is necessary to raise the level of social work studies and research, both *from* social workers and *about* social work, since they are generally carried out by other professionals. There is a need to research daily practice and conceptualize it so that it may be applied and generalized.

The lower academic level of the social work diploma is another factor that hinders social work. It should be modified to lead to a bachelors degree and PhD. This would in turn increase research and analysis about the profession and its effects, as well as enriching knowledge on epidemiology and care.

The challenges of the European social order, new emerging needs and new forms of partnership will together lead to the creation of a new, innovative social work, linked to initiatives and projects by ordinary people, making use of public and private social services and resources. Such initiatives might enable private practice to emerge, and emancipate social work from social services and from professional teams that entangle it in many cases. Finally, many young workers show considerable interest and skill in social work practice, and we hope that they will contribute new perspectives to the profession.

9 Social work in the United Kingdom

Steven Shardlow, Tim Robinson, Jo Thompson and June Thoburn

Introduction

It is perhaps best to acknowledge at the outset the impossibility of describing briefly and simply the context of modern social work in the United Kingdom and of outlining recent significant changes in policy and practice. However, to provide something of use to the reader who wants to know about social work in the UK, we have been highly selective and have concentrated upon four major areas of interest: care for adults in the community; social work with children and families; probation practice with offenders, and social work education. In selecting these areas and presenting them, we inevitably ignore large and significant elements of social work policy and practice. We ask readers to be charitable in their expectations, and if we arouse interest or curiosity to find out more about social work in the UK, then we have achieved our ambitions. Before reviewing each of these specified areas, we have provided some background information about the UK.

The context of social work in the UK

According to some commentators, in particular government spokespeople, the UK has been the most successful economy in Western Europe since 1979. This success has allegedly been built upon a triad of: restructuring the context of work through the removal of restrictive labour practices; high inward investment from outside the EU, and reducing government financial commitments, for example in the field of social welfare. These changes that have affected financial, manufacturing and social structures of the UK have been implemented as a result of what are often referred to as 'new right ideologies', which have influenced, or as some might say, dominated government policy since 1979. In a recently-published book, Hutton undertakes a comprehensive if controversial analysis of the state of the UK (Hutton, 1996). He argues that the UK has been in serious economic decline since 1979, illustrated by, for example, the fact that in 1983 the UK trade in manufactured goods went into deficit – the first time this has occurred since the industrial revolution (Hutton, 1996, p.8) – or the fact that:

> more than half the people in Britain are living either on poverty incomes or in conditions of permanent stress and insecurity that has had dreadful effects on the wider society. (Hutton, 1996, p.109)

There are, according to this view, increasing levels of inequality in the UK, as measured by the distribution of income, and access to scarce resources such as health, education and the like. This is not the place to debate the true nature of the state of the UK. We can only illustrate that there are contested views of the current state of the UK economy and social structures. Readers must form their own opinion about the true condition of the state of the UK as a backcloth against which social services are provided.

Social services across the UK are highly diverse and varied. The four different countries that comprise the UK – England (population 48,707,000), Scotland (population 5,132,000), Northern Ireland (population 2,913,000) and Wales (population 1,642,000) (Central Office of Information, 1996) – have, to various degrees, different structures of local government, different relationships with the central government at Westminster, differing legal traditions generally, and different legislation in respect of social work, and different organizational structures for social services. Nor is this diversity confined to organizational and structural matters – cultural diversity among the population of the UK is considerable.

In 1994–95 £7.5 billion (a rise of over £1 billion over the previous year) was spent on the personal social services in England (Department of Health, 1996, Table 7.8). It must be remembered that the formal social services are not the sole providers of care – nor are they even the major provider. Care for those in need is provided informally by families and friends. It is difficult to estimate the amount of informal care, but the government accepts that the overwhelming majority of care is provided in this way (Department of Health, 1989a). As has been observed previously, the burden of providing care by family and friends falls disproportionately on women (Hallet, 1989; Langan and Day, 1992).

Social work has a long history in the UK, and its modern origins can be traced to the nineteenth century (for a full description, see Younghusband, 1981). It is not currently a regulated profession: anyone can call themselves a social worker. At various times during the past twenty years, there have been debates about the possibility of creating a regulatory body (with powers to set standards for practice and control entry into the profession) for social work in the UK that might lead to the creation of a fully-regulated profession. At present, following the publication of an influential report (Parker, 1990), there are active discussions involving governmental departments and key social services organizations about the establishment of a council for social services with full regulatory powers.

It is not easy to provide accurate figures about the number of social workers employed in the UK precisely, because there is no clearly-defined, regulated profession. According to the Department of Health, some 233,860 staff worked in the personal social services in England in 1995 – a slight reduction on the figure for 1994, 237,750 (Department of Health, 1996, Table 6.23).[1] Many of these people will be unqualified, especially those working in residential or daycare practice. There are about 63,000 people in the UK with social work qualifications (Smythe, 1996), but not all of these will be in work. According to recent research, about 20 per cent of those social workers currently working are men; despite the fact that a substantial number of social workers are women, over 70 per cent of managers are men (Balloch et al., 1995).

Social work is practised in state-funded bodies, such as local authorities and the probation service; in the voluntary sector, where agencies may receive grants but do not seek to make a profit, and in the private sector, where companies seek to earn a profit by providing services such as residential care or care in the individual's house.

In recent years, in response to government policy, there has been a growth in the quantity of social services provided by the voluntary and private sectors, leading to the use of a new term, 'the mixed economy of welfare', to describe the provision of social care within the UK. We would now like to review recent developments in key areas of social work practice.

Community care

For over a century, institutional solutions dominated the UK's response to the problems of people struggling to survive in the community with difficulties related to disability, old age and mental illness. In reality, even in the heyday of the institution, care in the community predominated, but it was largely hidden, provided, as now, by countless families, friends and neighbours with little support from public services. Gradually, though, as institutional provision has come under attack, community care has emerged into the open as the desired aim of welfare services and users alike. However,

---

[1] Note that these figures relate only to England – similar figures are available for the other countries within the UK, but here we are restricted in the amount of detailed information that we can present.

services to support users and informal carers in the community have been limited, fragmented and poorly-designed, and are concentrated in the public sector.

From the late 1970s, however, a series of action research projects sought to develop a new style of work in community care. This was called 'case management' or 'care management' (Challis and Davies, 1986; Department of Health, 1991a; Orme and Glastonbury, 1993; Ramon, 1992). Traditional approaches started from the available public services, and fitted the users into available services, whether they met their needs or not. Care management began from an assessment of what those needs were, and then looked at how these might be met in ways which were acceptable to the user involved. What was new was that care managers had devolved budgets, which enabled them to buy in services from outside their own departments and to encourage the development of new forms of support. As a result, for the first time, social workers had some real power over service providers, which made it possible for them to put together more user-centred, flexible and coherent packages of support, and to monitor and adjust these packages as the situation changed. Research comparing users who received a care management-based service with others who received more traditional services clearly demonstrated a range of positive gains for both users and carers (Challis and Davies, 1986).

The potential of care management was evident in a growing number of other demonstration projects (e.g. Challis et al., 1994). However, in the late 1980s, this new approach became entwined with the Thatcher government's concern to cut the growing cost to the state of residential care, and radically reform welfare along competitive market lines (Department of Health, 1989a). These ideas were incorporated into law in the 1990 National Health Service and Community Care Act. Social Services Departments (SSDs) may, in due course, cease to be the main providers of services and, instead, increasingly buy in what is needed on a contract basis from the voluntary and private sectors (Challis, 1990). Public money will remain the major source of funding but, over time, the role of SSDs will be restricted increasingly to planning, stimulating, managing and regulating a largely external and competitive market of care. In so far as SSDs continue to run any services themselves, these are likely to become independent cost centres, largely dependent for their survival on their ability to gain contracts from care managers in the same way as external providers.

In one sense, this new market-based system can be seen as a logical extension of some of the core features of care management as it was developed in the earlier experiments. These already implied a measure of competition between providers, and a greater use of external suppliers. However, if the government push their reforms through to their logical conclusion, it is clear that this will result in a radical transformation in the culture of social services departments, with the emphasis on a 'contract culture', rather than shared values grounded in social work practice. Embedding care management in such a framework is a massive social experiment whose consequences are, to say the least, uncertain. It is unclear how these markets will work in the long term, or whether social services departments will have the skills and experience or the technology to operate in such a system effectively (Wistow et al., 1994). Neither the experience of countries like the USA nor the literature on markets in other areas of welfare (Le Grand and Bartlett, 1993) give much cause for comfort.

What is clear is that for care management to fulfil its potential, it has to be the centre around which all else revolves. The process has to start from a comprehensive assessment of the individual user's and carer's needs, completed in partnership with them, and on which the care plan is based. The larger management structures need to be the servants of this process, not the masters. In turn, the overall planning of the SSDs' intervention in the market to stimulate new developments in services and to regulate the supply and quality of the services delivered to users needs to be based on information derived from the care management process itself, and subordinate to it.

However, the development of competitive, external markets in which the independent sector is preferred over public sector provision, a reliance on contracts as the means of ensuring the delivery and quality of services and restrictions on public sector spending point to a very different future. Many of the signs already point to the danger that these developments will warp the way in which care management is allowed to operate. Pressures are likely to build up on care managers and assessors to distort their assessments and care plans to fit in with these imperatives. Once again, users and carers will find themselves on the receiving end of services which are defined by professional activity rather than user requirements.

Clearly, assessors/care managers are on the fault line of this new system, and their commitment to partnership and user empowerment will have a profound effect on how users experience the system. However, it is far from clear whether care managers will be qualified social workers. Many departments seem to be devolving much of this work to lower-qualified staff, and employing relatively few social workers, particularly in work with older people. At the same time, there is a real danger that social workers will choose to avoid such jobs, as they are 'not real social work'. If social workers do abdicate the field, they may well leave it to others with far less understanding of oppression, and less commitment to user empowerment.

In all forms of care management, power still ultimately remains with the care manager and the agency. However, there is an alternative route which would more directly empower the user (Morris, 1993). The Conservative government briefly experimented with a direct payment scheme called the Independent Living Fund. Under this scheme, severely disabled people received cash payments which they could then use to purchase services direct. This allowed them to determine for themselves what support they received. The scheme proved too popular, and was eventually drastically reduced. Existing legislation prevents SSDs from making similar direct payments to users. However, an increasing number of departments are developing schemes to get around these restrictions. Under pressure from the Disability Movement (a loose confederation of interest groups and individuals), the government have now indicated that they will look at changes in the law which will make this easier. Although these schemes do not increase overall resources, they do allow the user to become, in effect, their own care manager. Where this will leave social work is not clear. Given this power, whether users will see any need to involve a social worker, or in what role, remains to be seen. This, perhaps, is the acid test of what user empowerment really means!

Social work with children and families

The England and Wales 1989 Children Act was implemented in 1991. It was accompanied by a set of principles for practice (DoH, 1989b), a summary of the research studies which had influenced the final shape of the legislation (DoH, 1991b) and several volumes of official guidance (DoH, 1991c; 1991d). There can be little doubt that fundamental changes in practice were intended. Indeed, the policies and practice of some local authority social services departments and some individual social workers had already been congruent with the Act even before implementation. For the majority, change has been slow, and day-to-day practice differs little from practice in the 1980s.

What, then, characterized that practice, and what changes did the Act seek to bring about? The emphasis in the 1980s had been on child protection and permanence policies as frameworks for practice. Underlying them was a reliance on 'quick-fix' ideologies. These found favour with agencies whose resources were being squeezed by a government determined to cut public expenditure, and were in keeping with public concern about child abuse, resulting in many more referrals of suspected cases of abuse, which had to be investigated. It is hardly surprising in this climate that 'permanence policies', usually interpreted as, 'If you can't get the children out of care quickly, termination of parental contact and placement for adoption will be the appropriate course of action,' were grasped as a way of getting through the workload. Also attractive were 'de-labelling' or 'down-tariffing' theories for practice, based on research which showed that social work services to young offenders had resulted in higher use of custody because earlier attempts at help were interpreted by magistrates as indicating that non-custodial sentences would be unlikely to succeed. A further influence on the 'quick-fix' thinking of the 1980s was the emphasis on 'technical' methods, such as brief, task-centred casework, or behavioural work which discouraged longer-term, relationship-based casework.

However successful these methods might be with families experiencing difficulties which can be clearly defined, the programme of Department of Health-funded research (DoH, 1995b; 1991b) gave clear evidence that, even if *parents* could be helped by packages of care and short-term social work methods, *children* who had suffered what the Children Act refers to as 'significant harm' would be likely to need a longer-term, relationship-based casework service. The research also indicated that some children were indeed successfully adopted from care, but that substitute family placement was the outcome for only a small minority of children in public care (Rowe et al., 1989), and that the risks of breakdown were higher than anticipated, with around 1 in 5 breaking down, and other children continuing to need a heavy input of therapeutic work, even after adoption, if the placement was to be maintained (Thoburn, 1990; Fratter et al., 1991).

In the light of these findings, the Children Act guidance emphasizes the importance of family support services and earlier intervention. Family Centres are recommended as a base for service delivery; providing practical help, including volunteer visiting schemes, advice and advocacy services, and the provision of daycare and out-of-home respite care or short periods of accommodation are encouraged alongside counselling and therapy. Children's rights and parents' rights and responsibilities are strengthened, and social workers are required to consult them about the nature of the service to be offered, and to attempt to work in partnership with them even when child protection is an issue (DoH 1995a; Thoburn et al., 1995). Family group conferences (Morris and Tunnard, 1996) are being introduced in some areas to attempt to shift the balance of power towards family members and increase the likelihood of partnership-based practice.

Examples of innovative support and early intervention strategies are beginning to appear in the literature, as with Bradley and Aldgate's (1994) account of respite care schemes for families under stress, and Tunstill and Ozolins's (1994) survey of the family support activities of voluntary sector child care organizations. However, Aldgate et al. (1994) and annual reports on the Children Act (DoH, 1994a; 1995b) have indicated that, with a few exceptions, agencies were reluctant to switch resources from crisis work, mainly centred on child protection allegations, to support for groups of families known to be vulnerable for a variety of reasons, including very low income, homelessness or mental ill health or disability.

Child protection investigations and assessments still take priority, though recent research suggests that therapy or support after the investigation and assessment is the exception rather than the rule (Hallett, 1995). An emphasis on criminal prosecution of the alleged abuser has led to the development of video interviewing of abused children for evidential purposes. This work, usually undertaken jointly with the police, has become a high-status specialism for child care social workers. However, research has indicated that it is often used inappropriately, and that very few successful prosecutions result (DoH, 1994b). Recent guidance from the Department of Health (1995b) suggests that it should be used much less frequently in more tightly-defined circumstances.

Another result of the prioritization of child abuse investigations and assessment has been that children looked after away from home have not always received the priority which their vulnerability within the care system demands if they are to be protected from future harm. The number of children on Care Orders or looked after on a voluntary basis reduced after the Children Act was implemented, and although numbers have risen again, they are still lower than in 1990. In response to research (summarized in Thoburn, 1994) about their vulnerability due to placement breakdown or abuse by individuals or the system itself, the Department of Health has been piloting a monitoring system to attempt to ensure that high-quality parenting is provided for children looked after away from home (Ward, 1995).

In 1995, a series of research studies was published which confirmed the trends described here and previously identified by the Audit Commission (1994) as failing to provide 'value for money' in terms of child and parent mental, physical and social health (Dartington Social Research Unit, 1995). The government intends to continue in its attempt to shift more resources into earlier intervention and a less confrontational style in child care cases.

Social work and the Probation Service

The Probation Service in England and Wales is made up of 55 Area Probation Services; these services relate to local government/administrative/geographical areas which may be coterminous with counties (e.g. Nottinghamshire, Hereford & Worcester, Gwent) or with the large metropolitan authorities (e.g. Merseyside, Greater Manchester). It is not therefore a 'national' service: area services, differing in size and in the complexity of their social composition, have been able to respond locally in structuring the delivery of services to their communities. Local Probation Committees perform the employer role, and have responsibility for appointments, pay and performance of staff, and are accountable to the Home Secretary for the strategic direction of their services. The Chief Probation Officer in each service carries executive responsibility and is accountable to the Probation Committee. The policy direction, aims and objectives of the service are subject to pressure from the philosophy, values and 'vision' of different governments, as expressed through different Home Secretaries and the

Probation Division at the Home Office. There have been seven Home Secretaries during the last 17 years of Conservative government (since 1979).

In order to have any understanding of the impact on the service of government policies – problems of reduced budgets, the drive for increased efficiency and effectiveness, continuing new legislation concerning the criminal justice system and sentencing, and a political public shift to punishment in the community – it is necessary to 'contextualize' the Probation Service in terms of its aims, values and personnel.

The Probation Service grew from court-based missionaries, early in the 1900s, entrusted with the task of befriending offenders and, through offering advice, assistance and friendly support, promoting rehabilitation. Probation has evolved into a professional, qualified service with a particular rehabilitative role to play on behalf of the state, within the criminal justice system of England and Wales (different structures apply in Northern Ireland and Scotland). Over the years, government policy, and resulting legislation, has endorsed the aims of the Probation Service and the rehabilitative ideals upon which the service was founded. The following values, coupled with sound theoretical knowledge, inform the objectives of the service:

- to seek an understanding and explanation of the underlying causes of a person's behaviour, whether structural, personal, socio-economic or psychological;
- to work on these 'causes' in a belief that people can change, can take responsibility for their behaviour, and can be rehabilitated.

During the 1990s, it has become evident that the government has long-term objectives to develop legislation and policy that reflects a real and significant shift in the underlying ideology, culture, personnel and work methods of the service, in order to create a different kind of Probation Service. Publicly, this objective is carried forward in statements which move the service from working with clients' offending behaviour in order to *rehabilitate* them, to the effective delivery of *punishment* in the community through tough and demanding sentences, which have the 'confidence of the courts and public', and which protect the public through the medium of punishment and discipline (e.g. Home Office, 1996). This long-term plan has been implemented via different mechanisms:

- an increased use of media and political platforms in order to stress the government's tough stand on crime and its sympathetic approach to all victims; this tough image is achieved by attacks on the Probation Service's work, methods, values, and also to suggest that the service is a 'soft option' for offenders, and not 'tough enough' on them (they are presented as being in need of discipline); further, probation officers are criticized as a group and as placing a misguided emphasis on the offender, rather than on any actual or potential victims;

- an increased holding to account of services via the Home Office's three-year plans, which lay down the key performance indicators for services, and the targets for their achievement;

- the development of key performance indicators themselves, which concern the time taken to deliver pieces of work (and thus the cost) or the rate of breach of court orders by probation officers and the compliance of services with national standards – these are a set of standards for the delivery of service applied to all probation services (Home Office, 1992; 1995);

- the development of the capacity to change the structure of services through the introduction of different grades of worker into the service grading structure, and the introduction of performance-related pay;

- the generation of pressures on area services to restructure according to financial imperatives, for example when budgets were cut drastically in 1995–96;

- the introduction of cash limit formula funding for the service (through which services are financed), which increasingly encourages services to shift priorities away from meeting client need to increasing the numbers of reports and orders or statutory, not voluntary, contacts with clients, etc.;

- the introduction of a case recording and management system at a cost of £110 million, which has the potential to change the nature of officers' jobs, increase redundancies and shift patterns of spending such that resources are taken away from the direct service provided to offenders, courts, victims, etc.;

- a plethora of criminal justice legislation – the 1991 and 1993 Criminal Justice Acts, the 1994 Criminal Justice and Public Order Act, and the training and changes in service systems which have been needed to deliver the legislation;

- the introduction of national standards (Home Office, 1992; 1995) under a banner of delivering tougher, more demanding community sentences, but which misunderstood the fundamental nature of the relationship between clients and probation workers;

- the incessant undermining of probation staff's confidence and job security by budgets cuts, service re-organization, redundancies, national standards of 1992 and 1995, Criminal Justice Acts, increasing

workloads, and lack of support internally through service organizations and externally through the press, television and radio from the
Home Secretary and Home Office.

The compound effect of all of these changes has been significant and trau-
matic for the Probation Service, and for those who work within the service.

In order to change the service fundamentally into a punishment agency
(Home Office, 1995), the nature of the people who are employed in probation
work has had to change. The Home Secretary consequently ordered a review
of the pre-qualifying training of probation officers. The campaign to retain
the existing qualification for probation officers and its status as a higher
education diploma provided through externally (i.e. outside the Probation
Service) validated courses is well documented elsewhere (Pierce, 1996). The
determination of the Home Secretary to remove the requirement for probation officers, on appointment, to hold the Diploma in Social Work (DipSW) or
equivalent professional qualification – against advice from almost every
quarter – must be viewed as a determination to achieve a substantial alter-
ation in the nature of the service by changing personnel (i.e. encouraging
more ex-army or police officers to become probation officers) – making
possible the desired shift in culture and working methods. The Probation
Service has always employed ex-army and ex-Prison Service personnel, as it
has also always employed ex-Church personnel and ex-offenders, but they
have had (and thus so have the clients and the public) the benefit and protection of a necessary training in theory and practice through which to best use
their skills and talents. The removal of the training requirement begins the
separation of the terms 'social worker' and 'probation officer', and thus
reinforces the shift from working with people on the causes of their offending
behaviour to enforcing punishment in the community.

Changes in service structure, organization, financing, personnel and culture are inevitable in order to deliver the legislative framework and policy
designed by the government since the late 1980s and 1990s. Criminal justice
legislation concerning crime, punishment and protecting the public was
drafted at a time when there was some concern about the inexorable rise in
the prison population, its cost in financial terms, and failures in terms of
reconviction rates, and reflected a wish to punish within the community.
The 1991 Criminal Justice Act turned the Probation Order into a sentence:
previously, a Probation Order was an alternative to a sentence. This subtle
change affects the way Probation Orders are perceived – now they are seen as
punishment, not as an alternative to punishment whereby help is offered to
the offender.

The Act also sought to move the prison sentence away from being the
central plank of the sentencing framework, with other disposals as alternatives. The intention was to send only those people to prison who deserved, by

nature of their current offence, to go there: their offences were 'so serious' that no other sentence could be justified or could protect the public. This framework thus moved, in theory, the non-custodial sentence to centre stage. At the same time as this fundamental shift was taking place, the notion of 'just deserts' also took hold: that offenders should be sentenced for their *current* offence, in the main, rather than on the basis of previous convictions (section 29 of the 1991 Criminal Justice Act), and that before a custodial or community sentence was passed, a pre-sentence report (PSR) should be requested by sentencers (except for indictable-only cases). A unit fine system was also introduced in the magistrates' court: this was welcomed by the majority of court users as a fairer system, more likely to prove workable in the enforcement of fines. The 1991 Criminal Justice Act introduced fundamental changes to the prison sentence, introducing automatic and discretionary release, and it brought in a new order: the Combination Order, made up of Probation and Community Service Orders.

At the same time as the 1991 Criminal Justice Act was implemented (in October 1992), the Home Office published national standards for the Probation Service. These were launched as a framework for more demanding community sentences, within which the Probation Service would deliver a more consistent service to users.

Before nine months' trial of the legislation had passed, the sentencing framework was radically undermined by the 1993 Criminal Justice Act. This legislation abandoned the unit fine system and the 'just deserts' principle, because the section of the 1991 Act which minimized the taking into account of previous convictions when sentencing was abolished. In 1994, the Criminal Justice and Public Order Act not only brought squatters, Travellers and party-goers into the criminal justice arena, but by an amendment took away the requirement for a current pre-sentence report to be ordered and considered before sentencing to either prison or community service. A year after the 1992 national standards were published, the Home Office had reviewed their implementation, and in March 1995 published new national standards, intended to be crisp, measurable and capable of offering consistent and demanding punishment in the community. Their emphasis was on the management of risk, and protection of the public.

Continued changes to the 1991 legislation, and increased insistence on notions of punishment and breach enforcement within national standards, have attempted to move the service from rehabilitation to punishment as a way of protecting the public. This ethos shifts the Probation Service's role from making demands on offenders by motivating them to change, to making demands on their liberty in the hope that punishment in this way will deter them. The Green Paper issued in March 1995, *Strengthening Punishment in the Community* (Home Office, 1995), was designed to supply community sentences in which probation officers would hold and manage a case without the need for ongoing supervision, risk assessment or contact; work on the offending behaviour would be ordered by the court and carried out by agencies outside the service. The ideological underpinnings of the Green Paper, translated into legislation, would have comprehensively changed the nature of the service's role, and its relationship with its clients, courts and offenders. The government did not proceed to the next stage of a White Paper. However, the Green Paper was discussed at a seminar convened by the Magistrates' Association and attended by representatives of those bodies involved in the sentencing process: members of the Central Probation Council, Association of Chief Officers of Probation, Justices' Clerks, the Judiciary, NAPO and the Home Office. The Home Office listened to calls by sentencers and others for a halt to further legislative changes, and picked up on an idea which emanated from the seminar: to improve the level of communication between the Probation Service and sentencers about their objectives and methods of work.

This has turned into the Green Paper Demonstration Projects, currently in place in Shropshire and Cleveland. The projects are designed to test how far some of the changes contained in the Green Paper can be initiated within current legislation and can 'increase sentencer and public confidence in community sentences and the effectiveness of those sentences' (Shropshire Probation Service leaflet, *Community Sentence Demonstration Project*).

These projects have only recently been launched (1997 in Shropshire) and may fold or continue quietly through the next wave of legislation proposed by the Home Office incumbents under a Labour government.

The 1990s have brought the spectre of a Probation Service charged with providing more for less, appointing unqualified personnel to manage large caseloads of increasingly difficult people. The fulfilling, quality work will be done more cheaply within the independent sector, and the service's role will be reduced to monitoring offenders under house arrest, and taking them back to court when, inevitably, they breach their orders.

Social work education

There is a well-established tradition of professional education for social workers in the United Kingdom. The first recognizable course for one branch of the profession, psychiatric social workers, was started at the London School of Economics in 1929. However, it was not until 1954 that the first generic course for those wishing to enter the full range of branches of social work (probation, child care, medical and psychiatric social workers) was created – again at the London School of Economics (sadly, and for many symbolic of the present situation of social work education, this course closed in 1995). Since then, the number of basic professional courses for social workers located within higher education has expanded considerably.

Besides the established tradition of university-based professional education for social work, a national body, CCETSW (Central Council for
Education and Training in Social Work), exists. CCETSW is an independent
body created in 1971 by government statute, and is charged with the responsibility for setting standards, approving and reviewing courses and inspect-
ing social work educational provision to ensure that required standards are
met. In addition, CCETSW acts as a developmental body to initiate and promote various activities that further social work education (e.g. conferences,
developmental workshops and publications). The existence of a national
body with substantial powers to determine the overall shape of social work
education gives a distinct and unique character to the nature of social work
education in the United Kingdom. Some regard CCETSW as the bastion of
national standards, while others see it as a meddlesome and interfering body
that seeks to impose a dull uniformity on social work education within the
United Kingdom. This is not the place to debate the impact and merits of
CCETSW. It does, however, have a substantial budget from central government, currently in excess of £25 million per year.

In 1989, a new professional qualification for social work was introduced,
the DipSW (Diploma in Social Work) – usually a two-year full-time course.
There are now (1997) some 122 DipSW courses. In 1995/96, 4,716 students
successfully obtained the DipSW, which is a comparable figure to previous
years (CCETSW, 1996). The provision of social work education is complex, as
the professional qualification, the DipSW, may be offered in conjunction with
academic qualifications of varying level: non-graduate, bachelors or masters.
This complex linkage between the national professional qualification for
social work and levels of academic awards defies either rational explanation
or justification. The system persists because, on a day-to-day level, these
anomalies are ignored.

The DipSW was introduced largely on account of growing dissatisfaction,
especially among employers, about the practical relevance of the existing
social work qualifications. This new qualification provided a unified professional qualification replacing the two previous major qualifications, the
CQSW (Certificate of Qualification in Social Work) and the CSS (Certificate in
Social Service). Prior to 1989, the bifurcation of social work qualifications had
been divisive – for example, the CSS was more likely to be obtained by those
working as assistant social workers and residential care workers, while the
CQSW was the dominant qualification for field social workers. Moreover,
there were often considerable differences in the ways the two qualifications
were provided, the CSS being mainly provided through day release to
employed staff, and the CQSW by full-time courses.

The DipSW introduced major new features to the landscape of professional
social work education.

First, the DipSW was linked to a specific academic level of education. In academic terms, the DipSW is equivalent to the level of work that is expected at the end of the second year of a three-year bachelors degree (this is despite the linkage of the award with different levels of academic award). Although this constitutes progress in clearly linking the professional qualification to a particular academic level, it also represents a major failure by the social work establishment – especially CCETSW – because prior to the introduction of the DipSW, strong arguments had been advanced by many sections of the social work education establishment that the new DipSW should be a three-year qualification, and should be at the level of a bachelors degree. This argument was lost, principally because the government refused to provide the additional funding required for a three-year qualification. This decision not to proceed with a three-year qualification has left social work in an uncomfortable position. Similar professions, such as nursing, are in the process of creating a graduate profession through 'Project 2000'. In addition, there has been a massive expansion in the numbers of students attending university education – now approximately 1 in 3 of all 18-year-olds. Given the changes in the educational structure of the UK and the nature of social work, it is difficult to sustain the argument that professional education for social work should not be at the level of a bachelors degree. It is difficult to avoid the conclusion, given the long tradition of social work education in universities, that professional social work has been unsuccessful in establishing a suitable structure for professional education.

Second, CCETSW requires that the DipSW is provided by a partnership consisting of at least one social work agency and one university or institute of education; the intention is to ensure that academic and professional interests are centrally represented in all social work courses, and that social work students are fully prepared for the world of social work practice. The results of this development have varied throughout the country. In some areas, very effective partnerships have rapidly emerged; in others, there have been substantial difficulties in bringing together different types of institutions. These partnerships are all unique: some have one university and several agencies; others consist of several universities and agencies, whilst others may comprise only one university and one social work agency. Some features of social work education can be more effectively delivered using such a system, but there is a price to be paid. The development of viable partnerships inevitably entails an increased commitment, by all staff involved, to joint planning, better communication and an increased number of meetings.

Third, the regulations for the DipSW (CCETSW, 1991) emphasize the importance of outcomes in education, rather than the processes whereby those outcomes are achieved. Hence, the regulations are prescriptive about the knowledge, skills and values that social work students must be able to demonstrate at the point of qualification of the DipSW. This represents a major shift from previous requirements for professional education.

Moreover, this trend, evident in other forms of professional education, has been carried even further in a review into social work education conducted by CCETSW at the government's behest. As a consequence of the review, more elaborate prescription of the outcomes of social work education has been made, and all courses are being required to undertake major revisions within five years of introducing the DipSW (CCETSW, 1995). There is a widely-held view among the providers of social work education that this review took place too soon, and that insufficient opportunity had been given to allow the system of social work education to settle after the introduction of the DipSW in 1989.

A major innovation created by CCETSW since 1990 has been the development of a framework for post-professional education (CCETSW, 1990). This framework consists of two new professional qualifications, the PQSW (Post-Qualifying Award in Social Work) and the AASW (Advanced Award in Social Work). The PQSW is equivalent to an academic qualification at bachelors level, while the AASW is the equivalent of a masters degree. It is intended that candidates for these awards will undergo a range of educational and practical experiences. Through these activities, candidates accumulate credits towards the qualification. The final award is obtained through the submission of a portfolio of work that demonstrates that the candidate has achieved all of the required competencies. During the period that candidates are working for the awards, they have a mentor, a suitably-qualified person who assists and advises them in the production of their portfolio. As of March 1996, over 2,350 social workers were actively registered for these awards (CCETSW, 1996). As with the basic-level professional qualification, the DipSW, these awards must be provided through a consortium of agencies and universities. However, these are not necessarily the same consortia as provide the DipSW; generally, they are larger groupings, and cover substantial regions of the country – there are some twenty consortia for post-qualifying awards. In two areas of practice there are recognized national awards (these fit into the framework described above, and provide credits towards the PQSW). One of these awards is the Award in Mental Health, for social workers who may be involved in the procedures for compulsory removal from the community of people with mental illness, and the subsequent enforcement of treatment if necessary. The other award is in Practice Teaching, for practitioners who teach social work students in agencies. That a qualification in practice teaching should be one of the first national post-professional qualifications demonstrates the substantial commitment by CCETSW to high-quality education for social work students.

Endword

In the early 1980s, there was a sustained attack on social work, exemplified by a polemical book entitled *Can Social Work Survive?* (Brewer and Lait, 1980). The grounds for this attack on social work are to be found in a series of mishandled child deaths and the failure of social work to define an area of competence unique to itself.

Yet again, similar voices are to be heard doubting the future of social work. There is popular distrust of and discontent with social work, if sections of the press are to be believed (Franklin and Parton, 1991). However, there is another danger to social work: that its professional territory will be usurped by other groups.

The Home Secretary has removed the requirement for a social work quali-fication for new probation officers, thus opening up probation practice to people without a social work background. The development of changes in the provision of care in the community has led to the development of care managers: there is rarely a requirement by employers that care managers should have social work qualifications. In the field of mental health, commu-nity psychiatric nurses are increasingly working in similar ways to social workers. Nor are these the only threats to social work practice: the develop-ment of the private sector is often associated with the payment of low wages and a reluctance to provide adequate training and education for those employed in this sphere.

The next few years will be an important time for social work in the UK. Social work must fight for the position that it has occupied, and must define and defend its role in a society that seeks to know the cost of everything, including the value of the contribution made by social work.

Please note that this chapter was written before the change of government in the UK, which occurred in April 1997.

10 Finding social work in Europe

Steven Shardlow and Malcolm Payne

Comparisons are odorous . . . (Shakespeare, *Much Ado About Nothing*, act III, scene V, line 15)

Introduction

In the opening chapter of this book we stated that it is not possible to 'know' social work in nation states other than ones in which we live, have lived, or of which we have substantial and direct experience. Our knowledge of social work in our domicile state is qualitatively different to our knowledge of other states, because we experience it not only through the written word, but through direct immersion in the cultural heritage of society, and also – like as not – at some time in our lives as a consumer[1] of social services, or possibly as a person who works in an agency that provides social services.

In seeking to understand the nature, form and structure of social work in other states, we need to remind ourselves of this separateness, this difference between the nature of our understanding about social work in our own and in other states. Let us take an example. It is all too easy to assume that if apparently similar words and ideas are used in two states, they refer to the same entities and, even more beguiling, that these notions have similar force and meaning for people living in different states. It is possible that they do: it is equally possible that they do not! We are not arguing for solipsism (the view that the self is all that exists or all that can be known), but merely for caution when attempting to understand the experience of others. It is, after all, relatively easy to translate words from one language to another; it is quite another thing to translate meaning successfully.

[1] There is no satisfactory term to describe people who use social services. 'Consumer' is used here, but it could have been many other words, such as 'client', 'service user', etc.

When we do make the attempt to compare social work in different states across Europe, what do we find? Well, we are likely to find some differences between each state on account of our likely different cultural heritage, and also just because we may be looking for differences in the first place. It may be harder to identify significant similarities. We need to remind ourselves that there can be no definitive interpretation of social work in different parts of Europe, either in terms of the differences, similarities, its significance and, most importantly, the attribution of quality.

One function (not, in our opinion, a particularly desirable function) of a comparative social work analysis might be to seek to define good and poor social work, and furthermore, to formulate these judgements such that one state's form of social work is defined as being better than another's. Such rankings are evident in many spheres of life, often performing the function of self-affirmation at the expense of deprecating others. To engage in such a form of ranking is, we believe, to misunderstand the value of comparative social work. This is to be found not only in the understandings of the 'other', but also in the increase in our knowledge of our own national practice of social work, and the excitement of generating dialogue through which both may learn how to incorporate the best of another's practice.

Before looking to see what we might find by subjecting the chapters to a comparative analysis, we need to remind ourselves of the scope of the discussion – at least those of us who live in Western Europe, and perhaps those in other parts of the world also. Europe is a continent without clear boundaries. At various times, different organizational and political structures have occupied substantial parts of the geographical land mass bordering Africa and Asia, among them: the Roman Empire, Christendom, the Holy Roman Empire, the Napoleonic Empire, Eastern and Western Europe in the post-1945 settlement, and the European Union. None of these structures, however large, has encompassed all of the land mass from the western shores of the Atlantic to the Urals in the east, from the Arctic Circle to the most southerly beaches of the Mediterranean. Always, parts of Europe have been excluded. Europe is an evolving entity, mysterious and ever in search of itself. As characterized by Lorenz, 'Project Europe' is: 'a complex, contentious and often contradictory set of assumptions and principles full of hidden agendas' (Lorenz, W. 1994, *Social Work in a Changing Europe*, London: Routledge, p.4). This book only considers part of Europe, several of the states within the EU. The EU is not Europe, nor is Europe the EU.

In what way should we compare social work in the different states? Simply listing or drawing attention to the differences may be interesting, but need not be illuminating. To state that social work in Germany exhibits different features to social work in Spain, which is different again from social work in Italy, is of superficial interest. But surely we want to know more? How are these differences to be explained and accounted for? That suggests the need for a historical analysis, but that is too detailed an enterprise to be undertaken lightly. Explaining the developmental path that social work has taken in any one of the states, much less comparing that development to another state, would require a lengthy book in its own right. Certainly, any detailed analysis of the historical development of social work is beyond the scope of consideration here. However, even if detailed analysis of this nature is impossible in this volume, if the latter provides the impetus for further and more detailed comparative work, the aspirations of the authors of all the chapters will have been more than achieved.

If detailed historical explanations of differences in social work tradition are impossible in the available space, then perhaps we should search for similarities and seek to explain these – possibly in search of the *Zeitgeist* of social work. This may be a more promising line of analysis, but it does assume that there is a discernible spirit of the social work age – a problematic philosophical assumption in itself that we would do well to avoid.

A simple, if incomplete, solution to our dilemma about how to proceed with a comparative analysis is to ask a series of questions, and to explore how social work in the various states in this book have responded to the questions posed. This will not be a comprehensive analysis, but ought to advance our understanding a little. We have chosen to examine briefly the following three questions, which may provoke different responses in different states:

- What do social workers do, and can this be understood in relation to other occupational groups?
- What is the role of social work at the interface between the individual family and the state?
- What is the nature of the relationship between social work education and society?

The boundaries of social work

Social work is a notoriously difficult enterprise to define. Debates have raged – is it a profession, is it a semi-profession, just what kind of enterprise is it? The range of activities that might fall under the rubric of social work is large indeed. From the states represented in this book, it is possible to discern different forms of social work practice across the states, and some of these forms appear to be unique or highly distinctive to one state. These activities define the boundaries of social work with other professional groups, and thereby define and legitimize the activities of social work. For example, we may ask in Portugal, how do the pastoral responsibilities of teachers interact with the functions of social workers working with families whose children experience educational problems? Knowing that social workers operate in this field generates questions about how they work and the extent to which social workers and teachers co-operate – if at all – in their work with children and families.

Answers to these types of question begin to define the boundary between social work and teaching as a professional activity. It is highly likely that this boundary will be defined in different ways across the various EU states. Perhaps in some states there is considerable emphasis on this type of work, whereas in others there may be less. This is just one example of a professional boundary – in this case between teachers and social workers. There are other professional groups, such as psychologists or pedagogues, who may also be involved at this particular professional boundary. Locating such boundaries 'maps' the professional space occupied by social work – the resulting map helps to define those legitimate activities that are the stuff of social work and with which social workers might be concerned.

One of the most startling of these boundary questions is evident when considering the role of the social pedagogues in Germany and Denmark or the *educatori* of Italy. Such a profession 'social pedagogue' does not exist at all in some of the other European states, prompting immediate questions about the distinction between social pedagogy and social work if, as seems likely, the work done by a pedagogue in one country might be done by a social worker in another, and vice versa. Given the apparent closeness of occupational space between these two groups, how do they work together? Are there rivalries between the two professions? These questions are posed in the context of writers from the UK, a country that does not have social pedagogues. Someone from a country which does have this professional group is more likely to be concerned with questions such as, 'How do countries which do not have the profession of social pedagogy undertake the functions that are performed by pedagogues, or are these functions not performed at all?' In either case, the social work profession enjoys a different boundary, and social work practitioners may well work in different ways on different tasks – hence social work is differently constructed. For example, in Italy there are examples of *educatori* working closely with social workers in 'street work' with disadvantaged children. In states where there are no *educatori*, do social workers perform these tasks independently or in conjunction with other occupational groups? Or perhaps these tasks are simply not undertaken at all.

It is difficult enough to map the boundaries of a fixed land mass, but it is almost impossible if it is subject to shifts and changes in the coastline. Yet this is just what is occurring with respect to the boundaries of social work as new professions emerge. In the UK, a new profession, care management (responsible for planning care packages for vulnerable people living in the community), is emerging as a professional group. The professional boundaries between care managers and social workers are as yet indistinct and hazy.

None the less, their appearance marks a change in the nature of social work practice. We need to be aware of the constantly shifting and evolving nature of such professional boundaries.

The shape of social work's boundaries is influenced by an enormous number of factors: historical factors such as the strength and influence of other occupational groups; prescriptions of the state; the legitimate dreams of the population, and the self-perception of the social work profession about the scope and range of its activities. An interesting example of this occurs in the Netherlands, where there are tensions within the profession centring on the ability of social work to meet material need, as opposed to providing psychological or emotional care for individuals. The approaches taken in the Netherlands can be contrasted with those in Portugal, where social workers have been centrally involved in the provision of material help through anti-poverty social development programmes. By considering the boundaries of social work across national boundaries, we can see that social work occupies a similar occupational space, but not an identical one, in each of the states. It is therefore subtly but distinctly differently constructed and defined in these different states.

Further analysis might help to identify core elements of social work practice that are present in each of the states included in the book – if indeed there are any core elements to social work practice! If we could name and identify this core, we might take a step towards a better definition of the nature of social work practice that can be better defended outside the profession and more clearly understood by those who use social work.

Different structures: The state, the Church and the individual

Social work acts at the interface between the individual, family, Church and state. The timbre of social work practice, as revealed in the various chapters, well illustrates the nature and quality of this interface in the various states. In Portugal, for example, we learn that prior to 1974 the state abrogated any responsibility for social affairs to the Church, but since then, social work as a function of the state has become centrally involved in the country's major social problems, particularly the alleviation of poverty. In Ireland, social work has played a significant role in the move towards the secularization of what has been a theocratic state, through espousal of issues such as the protection of abused children. To varying degrees in other states, religious organizations provide help and assistance to vulnerable members of society. Therefore, the state may choose to become involved in the social problems of its citizenry, or it can ignore and leave them to other organizations such as the Church. The state also determines the degree of its involvement.

Other factors than the role of the Church are evident in influencing the nature of relationships between state and citizen. For example, the growth in importance and influence of neo-conservative ideologies has led to the promulgation of ideas of social retrenchment in many parts of Europe. A good example of this tendency can be found in Denmark, where the Nordic social model of welfare has been strong, yet recently extensive state welfare provision has been challenged both on financial and ideological grounds.

Denmark is by no means the only state to be affected by such ideologies – their influence has been particularly strong in the UK. In Spain, the belief by the government in universal state provision has been abandoned. We can recognize in many of the states an ongoing debate about the nature of the individual's relationship to others and the body politic.

Underpinning these tensions are differences of views among the various constituencies about the extent to which individuals and families are expected to be self-supporting or can expect to receive various forms of social help from either the state or the Church. These questions are fundamental, and reach deep into the core of the nature of state and society. We can see that social work is the instrument of the state in enabling or developing certain policies. But more than that, social work can and does have a role in defining the nature and content of these relationships between the individual, family, Church and state. When our understanding is grounded in a comparative analysis, based upon occurrences in similar states, arguments employed by social workers about the role of state, Church, family and individual are strengthened and enhanced, because they are better informed about possibilities and realities.

Social work education

Differences in social work education across Europe have been documented previously. A number of texts have described many identifiable differences between traditions of social work education across various European states in respect of curriculum content, course duration, length and type of student placements in social work agencies, and so on. However these differences are manifested, there is one common issue that confronts all states – how to answer the question, 'What is the desirable level at which to locate social work education?' Is education for social workers to be located within the universities, or at another educational level within the educational system?

How these questions are answered has considerable importance, because the type, nature and quality of education provided for prospective social workers will be shaped both by the level of education and by the traditions of the particular type of institution. For example, in some states, if social work education is located within universities, it may be difficult to provide extended periods of practice-based education in placement. Further, the prestige accorded to social workers as professionals may, in part, be determined by the location of their professional education, and whether or not this is based in a university. The significance of locating social work education within the university system will depend both upon systems of education for comparable occupational groups and the meaning of inclusion or exclusion from the university sector within any particular state.

These are complex issues, and they require exploration in the context of each particular state. Looking at several of the states described in this book, there has been a significant development in recent years. Social work education has been raised in status and incorporated within the university system in some European states: in Portugal in 1989, the colleges providing social work education were fully integrated into the national system of higher education, and they were empowered to award diplomas; in Spain, the schools of social work became part of the university system in 1982, although the level of professional award, the diploma, is low in comparison with other groups for whom the award is at bachelors level. A similar disparity is evident in Italy, where despite the recognition that the diploma granted by schools of social work is the equivalent of a university diploma, a degree is required to have access to career grades and the management positions in local government where many social workers are employed.

These apparent trends in some of the Southern European states towards the inclusion of social work education within the university system can be compared with the systems of social work education within some of the Northern European countries, such as the Netherlands and Germany, where there is an established structure of non-university higher education institutions (*hogescholen* in the Netherlands; *Fachhochschulen* in Germany). These institutions are mainly teaching institutions, not research-based, designed to provide education for professional groups such as social workers. Separating education for certain groups in this way can have many advantages. However, there are some difficulties, due to differences in the meaning of 'university' and the significance of university education. For example, it is difficult to obtain a job as a teacher without a higher research degree, but these are only awarded by universities, hence it is difficult for graduates of the *Fachhochschulen* to become teachers or social workers. As a consequence, social workers are taught how to do social work by non-social workers who have the necessary qualification.

This well illustrates the importance and significance for social work of locating the education of the profession at a particular level within the educational structure. We may well wish to examine the status accorded to social workers in different states and how this is, in part, a reflection of the levels of professional education. Hence, in some states the struggle to locate social work education at a particular educational level has broad significance for the profession and its role in society.

Endword

The questions we have asked may not be the ones you, the reader, would have chosen to explore, and there are many other areas to examine, such as:

- the response of society and social work to new social problems (for example, sexual abuse in Ireland and Spain);
- the problems of migration and exclusion (for example, the foreign workers in Germany or the Travelling communities in many states);
- the move to de-institutionalizing care (for example, in Italy or Ireland);
- the growth of partnerships between professionals and families in the field of child care (for example, in the UK and Denmark);
- the mobilization of the community (for example, in Portugal);
- the debates about the nature of generalist or specialist social work practice (for example, in the Netherlands).

These are just some of the areas that readers might choose to explore to gain a better understanding of the nature of social work practice in Western Europe.

Social work is both a national and an international activity. Practitioners and theoreticians of social work are subject to the particular historical tradition of the state in which they learn and practise their profession. They are also subject to international influences on the nature of social work. Within Europe, the influence of American social work has been powerful in the period since 1945. That influence may be on the wane, as a greater sense of professional self-confidence in social work is evident in many of the European states dealt with in this book.

One question for the future development of social work in Europe is to consider how far the profession will continue to be defined through different national traditions and practices, or how far the future will see a harmonization of theory and practice across the various states. Within the EU, there are pressures towards eventual harmonization, both in social work practice and welfare provision, as in other occupational areas. It may be that the development of the truly single market envisioned in the Maastricht Treaty will require, in the fullness of time, an equalization of social benefits and practices. We might wish to speculate about the speed of these developments, and also about the nature and form that they will assume. This book has examined recent developments in a sample of the states of the EU.

To return to the theme expressed earlier in this chapter: Europe is not synonymous with the EU. We need to consider developments in other

European states, and to that end look towards future publications in this series where social work in other European states will be explored.

Our final word must be to invite readers to consider: 'Which questions would *you* frame about social work in Europe?'

Bibliography

Chapter 1: Exploring social work in Europe

Armstrong, H. and Hollows, A. (1991) 'Responses to child abuse in the EC' in Hill, M. (ed.) *Social Work and the European Community: The Social Policy and Practice Contexts*, London: Jessica Kingsley Publishers.

Brown, K. (1994) 'A framework of teaching comparative social work' in Gehrmann, G., Müller, K.D. and Ploem, R. (eds) *Social Work and Social Work Studies: Cooperation in Europe 2000*, Weinheim: Deutscher Studien Verlag.

Lorenz, W. (1994) *Social Work in a Changing Europe*, London: Routledge.

Payne, M. (1996) *What is Professional Social Work?*, Birmingham: Venture.

Chapter 2: Social work in Denmark

Andersen, B.J. (1989) *Anbringelsesforløb – en registerundersøgelse af børn og unge anbragt udenfor hjemmet*, Copenhagen: Rapport 89(2), Socialforsknings-intituttet. (*Placement sequences – a register-based study of children and young people placed outside the home.*)

Christensen, E. (1991) *Trængte Familier*, Copenhagen: Rapport 91(8), Social-forskningsinstituttet. (*Families in straitened circumstances.*)

Christensen, E. (1992) *Omsorgssvigt? – En Rapport om 0–3-årige Baseret på Sundhedsplajerskernes Viden*, Copenhagen: Rapport 92(7), Socialforsknings-instituttet. (*Child neglect? – A report about children aged 0–3 based on the findings of visiting nurses.*)

Christoffersen, M.N. (1988) *Familieplejen*, Copenhagenn: Rapport 88(11), Socialforskningsinstituttet. (*Family placements.*)

Christoffersen, M.N. (1993) *Anbragte børns livsforløb – En undersøgelse af tidligere anbragte børn og unge født i 1967*, Copenhagen: Rapport 93(11), Socialforskningsinstituttet. (*The life course of children placed in custody – a study of children and youngsters born in 1967 previously placed in custody.*)

161

Egelund, T. (1995) 'Bureaucracy or professionalism? The work tools of child protection services', *Scandinavian Journal of Social Welfare*, 5(3), July: 165–74.

Ertmann, B. (1994) *Tvangsfjernelser: En analyse af samtlige tvangsfjernelser i Københavns kommune 1990*, Kolding: Kroghs Forlag A/S. (*Coercive placements of children: An analysis of all coercive placements in the municipality of Copenhagen, 1990.*)

Evalueringscenteret (1994) *Socialrådgiver–og socialformidleruddannelser*, Copenhagen: Evalueringscenteret. (*Social work educations.*)

Flex, K. and Koch Nielsen, I. (1992) *Kommunerne og SUM-programmet*, Copenhagen: Rapport 92(11), Socialforskningsinstituttet. (*The municipalities and the social development programme.*)

Folketingets (1988) *Betænkning af 23. juni 1988 om et sociaalt udviklingsprogram*, Copenhagen: Folketingets Socialudvalg. (*Order of 23rd June 1988 on the Social Development Programme*, Committee of Social Affairs, the Danish Parliament.)

Guldborg, P., et al. (1991) *Anbring mig ordentligt – om unges tanker, følelser og fantasier*, Copenhagen: Munksgaard. (*Please, place me properly – on young people's thoughts, feelings and fantasies.*)

Halskov, T. (1994) *Liden tue kan vælte stort læs – Om enlige mødre i EU – 3 eksempler: Danmark, Tyskland, Italien*, Copenhagen: Socialpolitisk Forlag. (*Little strokes fell great oaks – On lone mothers in the EU – three examples: Denmark, Germany, Italy.*)

Jensen, M.K. (1992) *SLUT-SUM: En sammenfatning af projekterfaringerne fra Socialministeriets Udviklingsprogram*, Copenhagen: Rapport 92(18), Social-forskningsinstituttet. (*The social development programme is brought to an end: A synthesis of the project experiences from the development programme of the Ministry of Social Affairs.*)

Jørgensen, P.S., Gamst, B. and Boolsen, M.W. (1989) *Kommunernes børnesager – en undersøgelse af forebyggelse, visitation og anbringelse i syv kommuner*, Copenhagen: Rapport 89(1), Socialforskningsinstituttet. (*The child abuse cases of the municipalities – a study of prevention, referral and placement in seven municipalities.*)

Jørgensen, P.S., et al. (1993) *Risikobørn: Hvem er de – hvad gør vi?*, Copenhagen: SIKON. (*Children at risk: Who are they – what do we do?*)

Løkke, D. (1990) *Vildfarende børn – om forsømte og kriminelle børn mellem filantropi og stat 1880–1920*, Holte: Forlaget SocPol. (*Erring children – on neglected and delinquent children between philanthropy and state 1880–1920.*)

Nielsen, B.G. (1986) *Anstaltsbørn og børneanstalter gennem 400 år*, Holte: Foriaget SocPol. (*Institutionalized children and institutions for children through 400 years.*)

Socialministeriet (1990) *Betænkning nr. 1212 om de retlige rammer for indsatsen overfor børn og unge*, Copenhagen: Socialministeriet. (*Ministerial Order No. 1212 from the Ministry of Social Affairs on the legal framework of the assistance and efforts for children and youth.*)

Socialkommissionen (1992) *De unge. Portræt af en generation i velfærdssamfundet*, Copenhagen: Socialkommissionen. (*Young people. A portrait of a generation in the welfare society.*)

Socialkommissionen (1992) *En god start. Forslag til en samlet uddannelses – og beskæftlgelsesindsats for de unge*, Copenhagen: Socialkommissionen. (*A good beginning. Recommendations for a coherent effort on education and employment for young people.*)

Uggerhøj, L. (1995) *Hjælp eller afhængighed: En kvalitativ undersøgelse af samarbejde og kommunikation mellem truede famillier og socialforvaltningen*, Ålborg: Ålborg Universitetsforlag. (*Help or dependency: A qualitative study of co-operation and communication between troubled families and child protection services.*)

Chapter 3: Social work in Germany

Baron, R., Brauns, H.-J. and Kramer, D. (1986) 'Education of social workers and social pedagogues in the Federal Republic of Germany' in Brauns, H.-J. and Kramer, D. (eds) *Social Work Education in Europe: A Comprehensive Description of Social Work Education in 21 European Countries*, Frankfurt am Main: Eigenverlag des Deutschen Vereins für öffentliche und private Fürsorge: 169–208.

Bausch, M. (1995) 'Sozialpädagogin/Sozialpädagoge, Sozialarbeiterin/Sozialarbeiter: Gesamtbetrachtung zum Beruf und zur allgemeinen Arbeitsmarktsituation', *Informationen für die Beratungs- und Vermittlungsdienste der Bundesanstalt für Arbeit (ibv)*, 1(4): 25–36. (Report by the German Labour Office concerning the labour market for social workers and social pedagogues.)

Brauns, H.-J. and Kramer, D. (eds) (1986) *Social Work Education in Europe: A Comprehensive Description of Social Work Education in 21 European Countries*, Frankfurt am Main: Eigenverlag des Deutschen Vereins für öffentliche und private Fürsorge.

Council of Europe, Steering Committee on Social Policy (CDPS), *1994/95 Co-ordinated Research in the Social Field*, Strasbourg: Council of Europe. (Final Report to be released in 1997.)

Fachhochschule Frankfurt am Main (1994) 'Europäisches Studienprogramm des Fachbereichs Sozialarbeit', *Informationen für die Beratungs- und Vermittlungsdienste der Bundesanstalt für Arbeit (ibv)*, 24(15): 2,195–201. (Report by the German Labour Office concerning a European programme of studies at the Fachhochschule Frankfurt am Main.)

Habermann, G. (1994) *Der Wohlfahrtsstaat: Die Geschichte eines Irrwegs*, Frankfurt am Main/Berlin: Propyläen Verlag. (*The welfare state.*)

Institut für Sozialarbeit und Sozialpädagogik (eds) (1994) *Informationsdienst zur Ausländerarbeit: Migration und Armut – Migrationsgewinner und Migrationsverlierer*, Frankfurt am Main: Verlag des Instituts für Sozialarbeit und Sozialpädagogik. (*Information service on working with foreigners: Migration and work – migration-winners and migration-losers.*)

Jörg, P. (1994) '62 Social Work Curricula on German Fachhochschulen with Respect to Human Rights Content', Berlin: Prorektor der Alice-Salomon FH Berlin. (Unpublished survey in the German language.)

Keller, A. (1994) *Promotionsmöglichkeiten von Fachhochschulabsolventen an Universitäten – Übersicht zum gegenwärtigen Stand und Ansatzpunkte für eine Weiterentwicklung*, Berlin: Fachhochschule für Technik und Wirtschaft. (Report on the possibilities for graduates of Fachhochschulen to achieve a doctoral degree at German universities.)

Kramer, D. (1983a) 'Das Fürsorgesystem im Dritten Reich' in Landwehr, R. and Baron, R. (eds) *Geschichte der Sozialarbeit*, Weinheim/Basel: Beltz Verlag: 173–217. ('The social care system in the Third Reich' in Landwehr, *History of Social Work.*)

Kramer, D. (1983b) 'Wohlfahrtspflege im Dritten Reich: Frauen in Beruf und Ausbildung', *Frauenforschung. Informationsdienst des Forschungsinstituts Frau und Gesellschaft*, 1(2): 49–58. ('Social welfare care in the Third Reich: Women in occupation and education', *Research on Women*, Information Service of the Research Institute of Women and Society.)

Kramer, D. and Landwehr, R. (1988) *Soziales Berlin* (English-language edn), Berlin: The Senator for Health and Social Affairs in connection with the Senator for Youth and Family. (*Social Berlin.*)

Landwehr, R. and Baron, R. (eds) (1983) *Geschichte der Sozialarbeit*, Weinheim/ Basle: Beltz Verlag. (*History of social work.*)

Landwehr, R. with Wolff, R. (1992) 'European handbook on social services in the Federal Republic of Germany' in Munday, B. (ed.) *Social Services in the Member States of the European Community: A Handbook of Information and Data*, Canterbury: University of Kent at Canterbury: 1–44.

Munday, B. (ed.) (1982) *Social Services in the Member States of the European Community: A Handbook of Information and Data*, Canterbury: University of Kent at Canterbury.

Salomon, A. (1983) *Charakter ist Schicksal: Lebenserinnerungen* (translated by Rolf Landwehr), Weinheim/Basle: Beltz Verlag. (*Character is destiny: Autobiography.*)

Wieler, J. (1987) *Erinnerung eines zerstörten Lebensabends*, Darmstadt: Lingbach. (In it Wieler remembers a destroyed last phase of life – Alice Salomon's.)

Wienand, M. (1988) *The Social System and Social Work in the Federal Republic of*

Germany, Frankfurt am Main: Eigenverlag des Deutschen Vereins für öffentliche und private Fürsorge.

Chapter 4: Social work in Ireland

Buckley, H. (1995) 'Training: the key to effective child protection service', *Irish Times*, 22 April: 5.

Cagney, M. (1995) 'Special Interest Group on Ageing', *Annual Report 1994–1995, Irish Association of Social Workers*, Dublin: IASW.

Clarke, B. (1991) 'The community care perspective', *Irish Social Worker*, Winter/Spring, 10(4): 13–15.

Curry, J. (1980) *The Irish Social Services* (1st edn), Dublin: Institute of Public Administration.

Curry, J. (1993) *Irish Social Services* (2nd edn), Dublin: Institute of Public Administration.

Curtin, C., Haase, T. and Tovey, H. (1996) *Poverty in Rural Ireland: A Political Economy Perspective*, Dublin: Oak Tree Press in association with Combat Poverty Agency.

Department of Health (1993) *Ad Hoc Committee on Social Work Qualifications*, Dublin: unpublished.

Department of Health (1994) *Shaping a Healthier Future: A Strategy for Effective Health Care in the 1990s*, Dublin: Government Publications.

Department of Health (1996a) *Putting Children First: A Discussion Document on Mandatory Reporting*, Dublin: Government Publications.

Department of Health (1996b) 'Minister for Health announces restructuring of health services in Dublin, Kildare and Wicklow', Press Release, 27 November.

Department of Health (1997a) *Statistics on Children in Care of Health Boards*, Dublin: Government Publications.

Department of Health (1997b) *Putting Children First: Promoting and Protecting the Rights of Children*, Dublin: Government Publications.

Donnelly, G.P. (1994) 'Managing child protection services in a rural context', *Irish Social Worker*, Spring, 12(1): 8–9.

Duffy, D., Fitzgerald, J., Kearney, I. and Shortall, F. (1997) *The ESRI Medium-term Review 1997–2003*, Dublin: Economic and Social Research Institute.

Duggan, C. (1991) 'A delicate balancing act', *Irish Social Worker*, Winter/Spring, 10(4): 11–12.

Ferguson, H. (1995) 'Child welfare, child protection and the Child Care Act 1991: key issues for policy and practice' in H. Ferguson and P. Kenny (eds) *On Behalf of the Child*, Dublin: A. and A. Farmer: 121-41.

Ferguson, H. and Kenny, P. (eds) (1995) *On Behalf of the Child: Child Welfare, Child Protection and the Child Care Act 1991*, Dublin: A. and A. Farmer.

Ferguson, H., Gilligan, R. and Torode, R. (1993) *Surviving Childhood Adversity*

– *Issues for Policy and Practice*, Dublin: Department of Social Studies, Trinity College.

Gilligan, R. (1991) *Irish Child Care Services – Policy, Practice and Provision*, Dublin: Institute of Public Administration.

Gogarty, H. (1995) 'The implications of the Child Care Act 1991 for working with children in care' in H. Ferguson and P. Kenny (eds) *On Behalf of the Child*, Dublin: A. and A. Farmer: 105–20.

Guthrie, B. (1995) 'Special interest group on Travellers', *Annual Report 1994– 1995, Irish Association of Social Workers*, Dublin: IASW.

Hegarty, M. (1993) 'Women deserve more', *Irish Social Worker*, Autumn, 11(4): 8–9.

Horgan, B. (1996) 'A Content Analysis of the *Irish Social Worker*', social work dissertation, Dublin: University College, unpublished.

IASW (Irish Association of Social Workers) (1997) 'Delegation to meet with Minister of State, Departments of Health, Education and Justice, May 1997' (informal communication).

Ireland (1996a) *Houses of the Oireachtas Interim Report of the Joint Committee on the Family* (Kelly Fitzgerald), Dublin: Government Publications.

Ireland (1996b) *Report on the Inquiry into the Operation of Madonna House*, Dublin: Government Publications.

Ireland (1996c) *Strengthening Families for Life, Interim Report of the Commission on the Family*, Dublin: Government Publications.

Ireland (1996d) *Partnership 2000 for Inclusion, Employment and Competitiveness*, Dublin: Government Publications.

Ireland (1997) *Support for the Voluntary Sector*, Dublin: Government Publications.

Irish Times (1995) 'Preventing child abuse', Editorial, *Irish Times*, 22 April.

Irish Times (1997) 'Expert predicts strain for social workers', 1 March.

Kelly, A. (1995) 'A public health nursing perspective' in H. Ferguson and P. Kenny (eds) *On Behalf of the Child*, Dublin: A. and A. Farmer: 186–202.

Kenny, P. (1995) 'The Child Care Act 1991 and the social context of child protection' in H. Ferguson and P. Kenny (eds) *On Behalf of the Child*, Dublin: A. and A. Farmer: 42–59.

Kilmurray, A. and Richardson, R. (1994) *Focus on Children: Blueprint for Action*, Northern Ireland: Focus on Children.

Kirwan, G. (1995) 'Special interest group on child care', *Annual Report 1994– 1995, Irish Association of Social Workers*, Dublin: IASW.

Lavan, A. (1991) 'The future of community care', *Partnership in Practice: The Future of the Personal Social Services*, conference proceedings, Limerick: Mid Western Health Board.

Lorenz, W. (1994) *Social Work in a Changing Europe*, London and New York: Routledge.

McCabe, A. (1996) 'Building Protective Systems: From Small Beginnings',

Paper to IPSCAN 11th International Conference on Child Abuse and Neglect, Dublin, Ireland, 18–21 August, unpublished.

McGrath, K. (1994) 'Supervision in social work: what do we want?', *Irish Social Work*, Spring, 12(1): 10–11.

McGrath, K. (1995) 'Adolescent sex offenders', *Irish Times Education and Living Supplement*, 21 November: 5.

McGuinness, C. (1993) *Report of the Kilkenny Incest Investigation*, Dublin: Government Stationery Office.

McKeown, K. and Gilligan, R. (1990) 'Child Sexual Abuse in the Eastern Health Board area of Ireland: an analysis of all confirmed cases in 1988'. Paper presented to Sociological Association of Ireland Conference, 3 March.

McKeown, K. and Gilligan, R. (1991) 'Child sexual abuse in the Eastern Health Board region of Ireland: An analysis of 512 confirmed cases in 1988', *The Economic and Social Review*, 22(2): 101–34.

McLellan, D. (1994) 'Who parents the children deprived of family life?', *Irish Social Worker*, Autumn/Winter, 12(3/4): 9–11.

Mid Western Health Board (1991) *Partnership in Practice: The Future of the Personal Social Services*, conference proceedings, Limerick: Mid Western Health Board.

Milotte, M. (1997) *Banished Babies: The Secret History of Ireland's Baby Export Business*, Dublin: New Island Books.

Moloney, C. (1994) 'Shared rearing with traveller families: A traveller solution to a traveller problem?', social work dissertation, Dublin: University College, unpublished.

O'Connor, J. (1991) *Speaking Out: A Study of Unmet Welfare Needs*, Limerick: Social Sciences Research Centre, University of Limerick.

O'Hearn, D. (1995) 'Global restructuring and the Irish political economy' in P. Clancy, S. Drudy, K. Lynch and L. O'Dowd (eds) *Irish Society – Sociological Perspectives*, Dublin: Institute of Public Administration.

O'Loughlin, A. (1995) 'Elder abuse: A perspective from Ireland', *Social Work in Europe*, 2(3): 24–29.

O'Morain, P. (1995) 'New guidelines may lead to rise in child abuse investigations', *Irish Times*, 22 April: 1.

O'Sullivan, E. (1995) 'Section 5 of the Child Care Act 1991 and youth homelessness' in H. Ferguson and P. Kenny (eds) *On Behalf of the Child*, Dublin: A. and A. Farmer, 84–104.

Richardson, V. (1994) 'The changing Irish family', *Irish Social Worker*, Autumn/Winter 12(3/4): 4–6.

Chapter 5: Social work in Italy

The theoretical basis of social work values, methods, techniques and training

Bernocchi, R., Canevini, M., Cremoncini, V., Ferrario, F., Gazzaniga, L. and Dal Pra Ponticelli, M. (1984) *Le scuole di servizio sociale in Italia: Aspetti e momenti della loro storia*, Padova: Fondazione E. Zancan. (*The schools of social work in Italy: Aspects and moments of their history.*)

Bianchi, E. (ed.) (1993) *Servizio sociale e lavoro con i gruppi*, Milan: F. Angeli. (*Social work and work with groups.*)

Bianchi, E., Cavallone, A.M., Dal Pra Ponticelli, M., De Sandre, I., Gius, E. and Palmonari, A. (1988) *Il lavoro sociale professionale tra soggetti e istituzioni*, Padova: Fondazione E. Zancan. (*Professional social work between subjects and institutions.*)

Bisleri, C., Ferrario, F., Giraldo, S., Gottardi, G. and Neve, E. (1995) *La supervisione: Orientamenti ed esperienze di guida dei tirocini professionali*, Milan: F. Angeli. (*Trends and experiences in guidance and supervision of students' fieldwork.*)

Bolocan Parisi, L., Gervasio Carbonaro, G. and Viciani Bennici, A. (1988) *Il lavoro di gruppo*, Rome: NIS. (*Group work.*)

Campanini, A. and Luppi, F. (1988) *Servizio sociale e modello sistemico*, Rome: NIS. (*Social work and the systemic model.*)

Cellentani, O., Facchini, F. and Guidicini, P. (1991) *Dimensione relazionale e sistema dei valori nel servizio sociale*, Milan: F. Angeli. (*The relational dimension and the value system in social work.*)

Centro Studi di Servizio Sociale (1991) 'Quale etica? Codice deontologico dell'Assistente Sociale', *La Professione Sociale*, No. 1, Bologna: Cluep. ('Which ethics?').

Commissione di Indagine sulla Povertà e sull'Emarginazione (1995) '*La povertà in Italia*', Rome: Presidenza del Consiglio dei Ministri.

Coordinamento Nazionale Docenti di Servizio Sociale (1987) *Il servizio sociale come processo di aiuto*, Milan: F. Angeli. (*Social work as a helping process.*)

Dal Pra Ponticelli, M. (ed.) (1985) *I modelli teorici del servizio sociale*, Rome: Astrolabio. (*Social work theoretical models.*)

Dal Pra Ponticelli, M. (1987) *Lineamenti di servizio sociale*, Rome: Astrolabio. (*Basic social work elements.*)

Ferrario, F. (1992) *Il lavoro di rete nel servizio sociale*, Rome: NIS. (*Working with networks in social work.*)

Ferrario, F. and Gottardi, G. (1987) *Territorio e servizio sociale: Aspetti e problemi di un intervento*, Milan: Unicopli. (*The local community and social work: Aspects and problems of a model of intervention.*)

Folgheraiter, F. and Donati, P. (eds) (1991) *Community Care: Teoria e pratica del lavoro di rete*, Trento: Centro Studi Erickson. [The book is in Italian. The title comes from the fact that the original literature in English influenced the idea and development of community care in Italy.] (*Community Care: Theory and practice in working with networks.*)

Fondazione E. Zancan (1992) *La supervisione professionale nel servizio sociale*, Padova: Servizi Sociali. (*Professional supervision in social work.*)

Lerma, M. (1992) *Metodi e tecniche del processo di aiuto: Approccio sistemico relazionale alla teoria e alla pratica del servizio sociale*, Rome: Astrolabio. (*Methods and techniques of the helping process: The systemic relational approach to social work theory and practice.*)

Martini, E.R. and Sequi, R. (1995) *La comunità locale: Approcci teorici e criteri di intervento*, Rome: NIS. (*The local community: Theoretical approaches and intervention criteria.*)

Milana, G. and Pittaluga, M. (1983) *Realtà psichica e realtà sociale: Una proposta psicoanalitica per i servizi sociali*, Rome: Armando. (*Psychic reality and social reality: A psychoanalytic proposal for the social services.*)

Neve, E. and Niero, M. (eds) (1990) *Il tirocinio: Modelli e strumenti nell'esperienza delle scuole di servizio sociale italiane*, Milan: F. Angeli. (*Students' fieldwork: Models and instruments in the experience of the Italian school of social work.*)

Ossicini Ciolfi, T. (1988) *Ricerca e servizio sociale: Dalle prime inchieste alle ricerche contemporanee*, Rome: NIS. (*Research and social work: From the first studies to contemporary research.*)

Sanicola, L. (1994) *L'intervento di rete*, Naples: Liguori. (*Working with networks.*)

Vecchiato, T. and Villa F. (eds) (1995) *Etica e servizio sociale*, Milan: Vita e Pensiero. (*Ethics and social work.*)

Areas of social work practice and some current issues

Ardone, R. and Mazzoni, S. (1994) *La mediazione familiare*, Milan: Giuffre. (*Family mediation.*)

Bianchi, E. and Dal Pra Ponticelli, M. (eds) (1994) *Storie di lavoro nel servizio sociale*, Milan: F. Angeli. (*Social work case histories.*)

Bortolotti, G., Galli, D. and Garavini, C. (1994) *Storie di servizi e di minori*, Milan: F. Angeli. (*Histories of services and children.*)

Campanini, A. (1993) *Maltrattamento all'infanzia: Problemi e strategie di intervento*, Rome: NIS. (*Child abuse: Problems and intervention strategies.*)

CISS, Ministero di Grazia e Giustizia (1993) 'Il servizio sociale nel Sistema Giustizia', in *Sviluppo e Servizi Sociali*, 2–3, Rome: Comitato Italiano del Servizio Sociale. ('Social work with offenders'.)

CISS, Ministero di Grazia e Giustizia (1995) 'Il servizio sociale nel Sistema Giustizia', in *Sviluppo e Servizi Sociali*, 1–2, Rome: Comitato Italiano del Servizio Sociale. ('Social work with offenders'.)

Civenti, G. and Cocchi, A. (1994) *L'assistente sociale nei servizi psichiatrici*, Rome: NIS. (*Social work in the psychiatric services*.)

Del Rio, G. (1990) *Stress e lavoro nei servizi*, Rome: NIS. (*Stress and work in health and social services*.)

Gardini, M.P. and Tessari, M. (1992) *L'assistenza domiciliare per i minori*, Rome: NIS. (*Home educational assistance for children*.)

Ossicini Ciolfi, T., Cipriani, R. and Pittaluga, M. (eds) (1995) *Aiuto e controllo nel servizio sociale: Una ricerca a Roma*, La Goliardica: Euroma. (*Help and control in social work: A research study in Rome*.)

Spinelli, E. (1995) *Se 'il matto' non sparisce: Dalla dipendenza all'interdipendenza nel lavoro dei servizi*, Milan: F. Angeli. (*If 'the madman' does not disappear: From dependence to interdependence in the work of health and social services*.)

Taccani, P. (ed.) (1994) *Dentro la cura*, Milan: F. Angeli [research on carers of older dependent people]. (*Inside caring*.)

Verno, F. (ed.) (1989) *Minori: Un impegno per la comunita' locale*, Padova: Fondazione E. Zancan. (*Children: A commitment for the local community*.)

Studies and research on the social professions

IRESS Regione Emilia Romagna (1990) 'Ruolo e funzioni dell'Assistente Sociale nell'organizzazione dei servizi socio-sanitari: nuove domande di formazione', in *Autonomie Locali e Servizi Sociali*, Bologna: Il Mulino. ('Role and functions of the social workers in the organization of health and social services: New education needs and requests'.)

Labos-Ministero dell'Interno (1993) *Le professioni sociali oggi*, Rome: Ter Editions. (*The social professions today*.)

Maurizio, R. and Rei, D. (1991) *Professioni nel sociale*, Torino: Gruppo Abele Editions. (*The professions in the social field*.)

Ministero dell'Interno (1988) *Professioni sociali e Universita*, Rome: Istituto Poligrafico dello Stato. (*The social professions and the university*.)

Ministero dell'Interno, Direzione Generale dei Servizi Civili (1983), *Gli operatori sociali. Urgenza di una normativa*, Rome: Istituto Poligrafico dello Stato. (*Professionals in the social field: The urgent need for legislation*.)

Niero, M. (1992) *Rapporto sulle professioni sociali*, Venice: Regione Veneto. (*Report on the social professions*.)

Chapter 6: Social work in the Netherlands

Broekman, J.M. (ed.) (1964) *Maatschappelijk Werk*, Amsterdam. (*Social work*.)

Cooper, A. and Pitts, J. (1994) 'Ironic investigations: The relationship between trans-national European social work research and social work education', in Gerd Gehrmann, Klaus D. Müller and Robert Ploem (eds) *Social Work and Social Work Studies*, Weinheim: Deutscher Studien Verlag.

Engbersen, R. and Laan, G. van der (1995) 'Rehabilitatie naar eigen vermogen', *Dagwerk*, Houten: Bohn Staflen Van Loghum. ('Rehabilitation according to one's own possibilities'.)

Laan, G. van der (1994a) 'Van turbulentie tot stroomlijning', *Sociale Interventie*, 4. ('From turbulence to streamlining'.)

Laan, G. van der (1994b) 'Hoe maatschappelijk is psychosociaal?' in Van der Laan, G. and De Goede, C. (eds) *Psychosociale hulpverlening in het maatschappelijk werk*, Utrecht: NIZW. ('How societal is psychosocial?'.)

Laan, G. van der (1995) 'The quality of information and communication', *Computers in Human Services*, 314, New York: Hayworth Press: 339–51.

Laan, G. van der and Potting, J. (1995) *Enige Cijers Over Werkdruk in het Algemeen Maatschappelijk Werk*, Rijswijik: Vog.

Melief, W. (1994) *Naar een dynamische benadering van arbeidsongeschiktheid en langdurige ziekte door het algemeen maatschappelijk werk*, Utrecht: Verwey-Jonker Instituut. (*Towards a dynamic approach of disablement and long-term illness in general social work.*)

Journals

In 1992 a new journal began publication under the name of *Sociale Interventie* ('Social Intervention'). [Its purpose is to study social issues and problems, and how to intervene in them. It is developing into a key forum for debate on social work issues.]

In 1994 the Netherlands Association of Social Workers (NVMW) launched the *Maatschappelijk Werk Magazine* ('Social Work Magazine'). [It is published bimonthly, and focuses on professional issues.]

From 1995 the *Welzijnsweekblad* ('Welfare Weekly') has been transformed into *Zorg + Welzijn* ('Care + Welfare'), which aims to cover a broader area, including the field of help and care. This is a more general magazine, carrying information about initiatives, conferences, publications, research projects, national and municipal social and welfare policy, and recent developments in the field.

Significant recent publications on social work and social work education

Behrend, E. (ed.) (1986–95) *Handboek voor het Maatschappelijk werk Ontwikkelingen in het beroep*, Brussels: Samson Alphen aan den Rijn (from 1986, published by Bohn Stafleu Van Loghum; from 1990, Houten in Antwerp) [annually-updated handbook for social workers].

Bruinsma, F. (1994) *Incesthulpverlening: Diagnostiek, opvang rn behandeling van incest*, Utrecht: Uitgeverij SWP [the latest overview of theories about incest and the treatment of incest victims and offenders].

Eggen, B., Jagt, N., Jans, J., Sluiter, S. and Wortman, O. (1995) *Methodiek maatschappelijk werk en Dienstverlening*, Houten/Diegem: Bohn Stafleu Van Loghum.

Gert, G., Müller, K.D. and Ploem, R. (eds.) (1994) *Perspectives of Social Work in Europe Europa 2000 Neuere Entwicklungen der Lehre und Forschung im Netzwerk Europäischer Zusammenarbeit*, Weinheim: Deutscher Studien Verlag (English texts of the Colloquium on Internationalization of German, English and Dutch Schools of Social Work, Frankfurt, 1993).

Hesser, K-E. and Koole, W. (eds) (1994) *Social Work in the Netherlands: Current Developments*, Utrecht: Uitgeverij SWP/Hogeschool van Amsterdam [an overview of different kinds of social work in the Netherlands].

Laan, G. van der (1990) *Legitimatieproblemen in het Maatschappelijk werk*, Utrecht: SWP [doctoral thesis about the way social work legitimizes itself in society with clients, other professions and the authorities].

Loo, J. van der (1994) *Hulpverlening aan jongens, een seksespecifieke benadering*, Utrecht: Hogeschool van Amsterdam Amsterdam/Soman [gender-specific social work with boys].

Ploem, R. (1992) 'Sexual orientation and the social work curriculum', *Issues in Social Work Education*, Spring, 11(2).

Ploem, R. (1994) 'The ecological perspective in Dutch tutoring/supervision', *Social Work in Europe*, 1(3).

Stouw, G. van der (ed.) (1993) *Maatschappelijk werk 3x: Theorie en Methoden Werkvelden Doelgroepen*, Groningen: Wolters-Noordhoff [teaching social work theory and methods, fields of social work, target groups].

Chapter 7: Social work in Portugal

Amaro, R.R. (1994) 'Desenvolvimento local em Portugal – as lições do passado e as exigências do futuro' (mimeograph). ('Local development in Portugal – the lessons of the past and the demands of the future'.)

Branco, F. (1991) 'Municípios e políticas socias em Portugal', *Intervenção Social*, 5/6, Lisbon: Lisbon Higher Institute of Social Work (ISSSL). ('Municipalities and social policy in Portugal'.)

Cardoso, A. (1990) 'Os novos desafios dos municipios promoção do desenvolvimento', *Desenvolvimento*, 5/6, Lisbon: IED. ('The new challenges of the municipalities in the promotion of development'.)

Costa, A.B. et al. (1985) *A Pobreza em Portugal*, Lisbon: Ed. Caritas. (*Poverty in Portugal*.)

Council of Europe (Social Committee) (1965) 'Functions, Training and Status of Social Workers in Member Countries of Council of Europe'.

Estivill, J. (1992) *Europe and the Development of the Mediterranean Welfare Systems* (mimeograph).

European Commission (1994) *European Social Policy – A Way Forward for the Union* (COM 94–333).

Ferreira, D. (1993) 'Que formação social em serviço social para os anos noventa?', *Intervenção Social*, 7, Lisbon: ISSSL. ('What kind of social training for social work in the nineties?')

Ferreira, L. (1994) 'Pobreza em Portugal – variação e decomposição de medidas de pobreza a partir de orçamentos familiares de 1980/81 e 1989/90', *Documentos de Trabalho*, Lisbon: CISEP. ('Poverty in Portugal – variation and changes in poverty indicators on the basis of family budgets from 1980/81 to 1989/90'.)

Gould, A. (1993) *Capitalist Welfare Systems – A comparison of Japan, Britain and Sweden*, London/New York: Longman.

Henriques, J.M. (1990a) 'Subdesenvolvimento local', iniciativa municipal e planeamento territorial', *Sociedade e Território*, 12, Oporto: Ed. Afrontarnento. ('Local underdevelopment, municipal initiative and territorial planning'.)

Henriques, J.M. (1990b) *Municipios e Desenvolvimento*, Lisbon: Escher. (*Municipalities and development*.)

ISSSL (Higher Institute for Social Work Education – Lisbon), 1994 Seminar 'Investigator o Agir' (Research or Intervention), Lisbon.

Netto, J.P. (1990) *Ditadura e Serviço Social: Uma Análise do Serviço Social no Brasil Pós 64*, São Paulo: Cortez. (*Dictatorship and social work: An analysis of social work in Brazil after 1964*.)

Nunes, M. H. (1989) '1992: Centre and peripheries, what social dimension?', (mimeograph).

Rodrigues, F. (1990) 'Social work education: A view from Portugal', *Issues in Social Work Education*, 10(1–2).

Rodrigues, F. and Henriques, J.M. (1994) *Pobreza é Com Todos; Mudanças Possíveis – Balanço de Uma Experiência*, Lisbon: Commission of the European Communities. (*Poverty affects everyone; possible changes – the balance sheet of an experience*.)

Rodrigues, F. and Sposati, A. (1995) 'Sociedade providência: Uma estratégia de regulação consentida', *Revista Crítica das Ciências Sociais*, 42, Coimbra: Centro de Estudos Socias (CES). ('Welfare society: A strategy of agreed-upon regulation'.)

Santos, B.S. (1990) *O Estado e a Sociedade em Portugal (1974–1988)*, Oporto: Afrontamento. (*The state and society in Portugal (1974–1988)*.)

Santos, B.S. (1991) *State, Wage Relations and Welfare in the Semiperiphery: The Case of Portugal*, Coimbra: Office of the CES 23.

Social Security Accounts (1990), Lisbon: Ministry for Employment and Social Security.

Sposati, Aldeiza et al. (1991) *Padrões de Reprodução Social na 'Sociedade Providência' – Estudo Comparativo entre a Sociedade Brasileira e Portuguesa*, São Paulo, Catholic University of São Paulo (PUC/SP) and Legião Brasileira de Assistência (LBA). (*Patterns of social reproduction in the 'welfare society' – A comparative study of Brazilian and Portuguese societies*).

Stoer, S. (1986) *Educação e Mudança Social em Portugal, 1970–1980, Uma Década de Transição*, Oporto: Afrontamento. (*Education and social change in Portugal, 1970–1980, A decade of transition*.)

Stoer, S. (1994) 'O estado e as políticas educativas: uma proposta de mandato renovado para a escola democrática', *Revista Crítica das Ciências Sociais*, 41, Coimbra: CES. ('The state and education policy: a proposal for a renewed mandate for the democratic school'.)

Recent publications

Andrade, M. (1992) *O Estado, a Sociedade e a Questão da Habitação em Portugal – 1960/1976*, PUC/SP and ISSS Lisbon (masters thesis in social work). (*The state, society and the housing question in Portugal – 1960/76*.)

Bizarro, M.M. (1990) *Mãe Não Há Só Uma: O Processo de Serviço Social Quanto ao Consentimento para a Adopção de Recem-Nascidos Numa Grande Maternidade Urbana*, PUC/SP and ISSS Lisbon (masters thesis in social work). (*There is more than one mother: the social work process in gaining consent for the adoption of the newly born in a large urban maternity*.)

Branco, F. (1993) *Municípios e Políticas Sociais em Portugal*, PUC/SP (Brazil) and ISSS Lisbon (masters thesis in social work). (*Municipalities and social policy in Portugal*.)

Carvalho, A. and Moura, H. (1987) *Serviço Social no Estado Novo*, Coimbra: Centelha. (*Social work in the new state*.)

Couto, B. (1994) *A Questão da Inserção Profissional dos Insuficientes Renais Crónicos e a Estratégia Terapêutica*, PUC/SP (Brazil) and ISSS Lisbon (masters thesis in social work). (*The question of the professional insertion of those with chronic kidney failure and therapeutic strategy*.)

Freitas, D. (1993) *Insucesso Escolar: Dupla Exclusão*, PUC/SP (Brazil) and ISSS Lisbon (masters thesis in social work). (*School failure means double exclusion*.)

Garcia, M.A. (1995) *Multiprofissionalismo e Intervenção Educativa: As Escolas, Os Projectos e As Equipas*, Oporto: ASA. (*Multiprofessionalism and educational interventions: schools, projects and teams*.)

Granja, B. (1995) *Adultos em Formação: Aprender ... Abrindo os Segredos da Vida*,

PUC/SP (Brazil) and ISSS Oporto (masters thesis in social work and social policy). (*Adults being educated: learning in order to open life's secrets.*)

Martins, A. (1994) *Génese, Emergência e Institucionalizaçao do Serviço Social Português – Escola Normal Social de Coimbra*, PUC/SP (Brazil) and ISSS Lisbon (doctorate thesis in social work). (*Genesis, emergency and institionalization of social work in Portugal – the Social Work Institute of Coimbra.*)

Monteiro, A. (1992) *A Formação Académica dos Assistentes Sociais – Uma Retrospectiva Crítica da Institucionalização do Serviço Social em Portugal*, PUC/SP (Brazil) and ISSS Lisbon (masters thesis in social work). (*The academic education of social workers – a critical retrospective look at the institutionalization of social work – Portugal.*)

Mota, E. (1995) *O Quotidiano do Idoso: Espaço de Regulação ou Emancipação*, PUC/SP (Brazil) and ISSS Lisbon (masters thesis in social work). (*The daily life of the aged: a space of regulation or emancipation.*)

Negreiros, M.A. (1992) *As Representaçõoes Sociais da Profissão de Serviço Social*, PUC/SP (Brazil) and ISSS Lisbon (masters thesis in social work). (*Social representations of the social work profession.*)

Nunes, M.H. (1992) *A Prática dos Assistentes Sociais: Uma Conversa Heurística*, PUC/SP (Brazil) and ISSS Lisbon (masters thesis in social work). (*Social work practice: an heuristic conversation.*)

Pinto, M.F. (1995) *A Cigarra e a Formiga – Contributos para a Reflexão do Entrosamento da Etnia Cigana na Sociedade Portuguesa*, PUC/SP (Brazil) and ISSS Oporto (masters thesis in social work). (*The cicada and the ant – contribution towards a reflection on the place of Gypsy ethnicity in Portuguese society.*)

Pinto, M.L. (1992) *Adopcões Ad-Hoc: Expressaõ de uma Politica Social para Criaucas de Familias Polies*, PUC/SP (Brazil) and ISSS Lisbon (masters thesis in social work). (Ad hoc *Adoptions: expressions of a social policy for the children of poor families.*)

Rodrigues, F. (1989) *Uma Abordagem da Especificidade das Questões da Habitação: O Caso da Área Metropolitana do Porto*, PUC/SP (Brazil) and ISSS Lisbon (masters thesis in social work). (*Looking at the specificity of housing questions: the case of the metropolitan area of Oporto.*)

Rodrigues, F. and Stoer, S. (1993) *Acção Local e Mudança Social em Portugal*, Lisbon: Escher. (*Local action and social change in Portugal.*)

Rodrigues, F., Nunes, H. and Teixeira, M.I. (1988) 'Pobreza: i) Dos pobres à pobreza ii) A pobreza em Portugal hoje iii) O serviço social e a pobreza', PUC/SP and ISSS Lisbon (mimeograph). ('Poverty: i) From the poor to poverty; ii) Poverty in Portugal today; iii) Social work and poverty'.)

Rodrigues, F. et al. (1993) *Enfrentar as Mudanças Económicas e Sociais a Nivel das Comunidades Locais*, Oporto/Dublin: ISSS Oporto and European Foundation for Improving Living and Working Conditions. (*Coping with social and economic change at the local community level.*)

Rodrigues, M.B. (1995) *Contributos de Abordagem Comunicacional Para o Estudo do Suicídio Consumado do Adolescente*, PUC/SP (Brazil) and ISSS Lisbon (masters thesis in social work). (*Contributions to a communicational approach for the study of adolescent suicide.*)

Salselas, T. (1995) *Politica Social e Velhice em Portugal: Mudanças e Permanências entre Estado e Sociedade*, PUC/SP (Brazil) and ISSS Oporto (masters thesis in social work and social policy). (*Social policy and ageing in Portugal: changes and continuities with regard to the state and society.*)

Silva, L.M.P. Ferreira da (1988) *L'Agression Physique Envers L'Epouse – Etude de Sociopathologie Familiale Realisée dans la Société Portugaise*, Paris: Ecole des Hautes Etudes en Sciences Sociales (doctoral thesis). (*Physical aggression towards one's wife – family sociopathology study carried out in Portuguese society.*)

Silva, L. and Rodrigues, F. (1994) *Condições de Vida e de Trabalho da Mulher Trabalhadora Têxtil na Bacia do Ave*, Oporto: ISSS Oporto and Federation of Textile Unions (FESETE). (*Living and working conditions of the female textile worker in the basin of the River Ave.*)

Reviews and publications

Do Serviço Social, Lisbon: Association of Social Work Professionals. (*On social work.*)

Estudos e Documentos, Lisbon: Portuguese Centre for Research into Social History and Social Work. (*Studies and documents.*)

Social Intervention, Lisbon: Lisbon Higher Institute of Social Work.

Other publications

Actas da Mostra de Serviço Social dos Anos 80 (1988), Oporto. (*The proceedings of the showcase of social work in the 1980s.*)

AIDSS *Serviço Social e Saídas Profissionais*, Oporto (Report of seminar organized by the Association for Research and Debate in Social Work). (*Social work and labour market insertion.*)

AIDSS *A Ética Profissional e o Serviço Social*, Oporto. (Report of seminar organized by the Association for Research and Debate in Social Work). (*Professional ethics and social work.*)

Chapter 8: Social work in Spain

Acosta, N., Casacuberta, P., Mercadé, M., Salvador, P. and Serrano, C. (1994) *Necessitats de centres residencials per a malalts psicótics*, Barcelona: unpublished. (*Need for residential centres for psychotic patients.*)

Aragonés, M.T., Brisé, E., Fernández, J. and y López, E. (1981) 'Asistencia psiquiátrica y salud mental en Catalunya', *Revista de Trabajo Social*, 81: 6–15. ('Psychiatric assistance and mental health in Catalonia'.)

Colomer, M. (1974) 'Método básico de trabajo social', *Revista de Trabajo Social*, 55: 5–72. ('The "basic method" in social work'.)

Departament de Justícia, Direcció General de Justícia Juvenil (1992) *El programa de mediació a Catalunya: Estudi avaluatiu de l'aplicació del programa durant l'any 1992*, Barcelona: Departament de Justícia, Direcció General de Justícia Juvenil. (*The mediation programme in Catalonia: Evaluation of its implementation in 1992.*)

Diputació de Barcelona (1987) *Plans generals de serveis socials. Pla general d'atenció a la infància i a la joventut*, Barcelona: Diputació de Barcelona. (*General social services plans: General plan for children and the youth.*)

Doménech, Rosa (1989) *Panoràmica dels Serveis Socials i el Treball Social 1939–1968: Documents de Treball Social*, Barcelona: INTRESS. (*Social services and social work panoramics.*)

Generalitat de Catalunya (1985) *Llei de 11 de juny de 1985 de protecció de menors*, art. 9 Barcelona: Generalitat de Catalunya. (*Children's protection law.*)

Heras, P. de las and Cortajarena, E. (1979) *Introducción al bienestar social*, Madrid: FEDAAS. (*Introduction to social welfare.*)

Jones, M. (1968) *Social Psychiatry in Practice*, Harmondsworth: Penguin Books.

Rossell, T. (1987) *L'entrevista en el treball social*, Barcelona: EUGE Hogar del Libro. (*The interview in social work.*)

Ubieto, J.R. (1994) 'Che vuoi? Reflexiones sobre la actualidad del trabajo social', *Revista de Treball Social*, 135: 24–42. ('Thoughts about today's social work'.)

Chapter 9: Social work in the United Kingdom

Aldgate, J., Tunstill, J. and McBeith, G. (1994) *Implementing Section 17 of the Children Act – the first 18 months*, Leicester: University of Leicester.

Audit Commission (1994) *Seen But Not Heard*, London: HMSO.

Balloch, S., Andrew, T., Ginn, J., McLean, J., Pahl, J. and Williams, J. (1995) *Working in the Social Services*, London: National Institute for Social Work.

Bradley, M. and Aldgate, J. (1994) 'Short term family based care for children in need', *Adoption and Fostering*, 18(4): 24–29.

Brewer, C. and Lait, J. (1980) *Can Social Work Survive?*, London: Temple Smith.

CCETSW (1990) *The Requirements for Post Qualifying Education and Training in the Personal Social Services* (Paper 31), London: Central Council for Education and Training in Social Work.

CCETSW (1991) *Rules and Requirements for the Diploma in Social Work* (Paper

30) (2nd edn), London: Central Council for Education and Training in Social Work.

CCETSW (1995) *Assuring Quality in the Diploma in Social Work – Part 1*, London: Central Council for Education and Training in Social Work.

CCETSW (1996) *Stewardship Report: 1995–96*, London: Central Council for Education and Training in Social Work.

Central Office of Information (1996) *Britain 1996: An Official Handbook* , London: Central Office of Information.

Challis, D. and Davies, B. (1986) *Case Management in Community Care: An evaluated experiment in the home care of the elderly*, Aldershot: Gower.

Challis, D., Chessum, R., Chesterman, J., Luckett, R. and Traske, K. (1994) *Case Management in Social and Primary Health Care*, Aldershot: Arena.

Challis, L. (1990) *Organising Public Social Services*, Harlow: Longman.

Dartington Social Research Unit (1995) *Child Protection: Messages from Research*, London: HMSO.

Department of Health (1989a) *Caring for People: Care in the Community in the Next Decade and Beyond*, London: HMSO.

Department of Health (1989b) *Principles and Practice in Regulations and Guidance*, London: HMSO.

Department of Health (1989c) *The Children Act 1989: Caring for People – Community Care in the Next Decade and Beyond*, Cm 849, London: HMSO.

Department of Health (1991a) *Care Management and Assessment: Practitioner's Guide*, London: HMSO.

Department of Health (1991b) *Patterns and Outcomes in Child Placement*, London: HMSO.

Department of Health (1991c) *The Children Act 1989: Regulations and Guidance Volume 2 – Family Support*, London: HMSO.

Department of Health (1991d) *The Children Act 1989: Regulations and Guidance Volume 3 – Family Placements*, London: HMSO.

Department of Health (1993a) *Children Act Report*, London: HMSO.

Department of Health (1993b) *Report of the Secretary of State on the First Year of the Children Act 1989*, London: HMSO.

Department of Health (1994a) *Children Act Report 1993*, London: HMSO.

Department of Health (1994b) *The Child, the Court and the Video*, London: HMSO.

Department of Health (1995a) *The Challenge of Partnership in Child Protection*, London: HMSO.

Department of Health (1995b) *Children Act Report 1994*, London: HMSO.

Department of Health (1996) *Health and Personal Social Services Statistics for England*, London: HMSO.

Franklin, B. and Parton, N. (eds) (1991) *Social Work, the Media and Public Relations*, London: Routledge.

Fratter, J., et al. (1991) *Permanent Family Placement: A Decade of Experience*,

London: BAAF.

Hallet, C. (ed.) (1989) *Women and Social Services Departments*, Hemel Hempstead: Harvester Wheatsheaf.

Hallett, C. (1995) *Interagency Coordination in Child Protection*, London: HMSO.

HMIP (1993) *The Criminal Justice Act 1991 Inspection*, London: Her Majesty's Inspector of Prisons.

HMIP (1995) *Dealing With Dangerous People: The Probation Service and Public Protection – Report of a Thematic Inspection*, London: Her Majesty's Inspector of Prisons/HMSO.

Home Office (1992 and 1995) *National Standards for the Supervision of Offenders in the Community*, London: Home Office.

Home Office (1995) *Strengthening Punishment in the Community: A Consultation Document*, London: Home Office.

Home Office (1996) *The Three Year Plan for the Probation Service 1996–1999*, London: Home Office Communication Directorate.

Hutton, W. (1996) *The State We're In* (revised edn), London: Vintage.

Langan, M. and Day, L. (eds) (1992) *Women, Oppression and Social Work*, London: Routledge.

Le Grand, J. and Bartlett, W. (eds) (1993) *Quasi-Markets and Social Policy*, Basingstoke: Macmillan.

Morris, J. (1993) *Independent Lives: Community Care and Disabled People*, Basingstoke: Macmillan.

Morris, K. and Tunnard, J. (1996) *Family Group Conferences*, London: Family Rights Group.

Orme, J. and Glastonbury, B. (1993) *Care Management*, Basingstoke: BASW/ Macmillan.

Parker, R. (1990) *Safeguarding Standards*, London: National Institute for Social Work.

Pierce, R. (1996) 'The present and future of social work and probation education', *Issues in Social Work Education*, 16(1): 64–76.

Ramon, S. (ed.) (1992) *Care Management: Implications for Training*, Sheffield: Association of Teachers in Social Work Education/Sheffield University.

Rowe, J., Hundleby, M. and Garnett, L. (1989) *Child Care Now*, London: BAAF.

Smythe, M. (1996) *Qualified Social Workers and Probation Officers*, London: Office for National Statistics [Survey of Social Workers and Probation Officers].

Thoburn, J. (1990) *Success and Failure in Permanent Family Placement*, Aldershot: Gower.

Thoburn, J. (1994) *Child Placement: Principles and Practice*, Aldershot: Arena.

Thoburn, J., Lewis, A. and Shemmings, D. (1995) *Paternalism or Partnership? Family Involvement in the Child Protection Process*, London: HMSO.

Tunstill, J. and Ozolins, R. (1994) *Voluntary Child Care Organisations after the 1989 Children Act*, Norwich: Family Support Network.

Ward, H. (ed.) (1995) *Looking after Children: Research into Practice*, London: HMSO.

Wistow, G., Knapp, M., Hardy, B. and Allen, C. (1994) *Social Care in a Mixed Economy*, Buckingham: Open University Press.

Younghusband, E. (1981) *The Newest Profession: A Short History of Social Work*, Sutton: Community Care/IPC Business Press.

Abbreviations

AASW	(UK) Advanced Award in Social Work
APSS	(Portugal) Association of Social Service Professionals
CCETSW	(Ireland & UK) Central Council for Education and Training in Social Work
CMV	(Netherlands) Cultural and Social Education
CQSW	(Ireland & UK) Certificate of Qualification in Social Work
CSS	(UK) Certificate in Social Services
DipSW	(UK) Diploma in Social Work
DoH	(UK) Department of Health – a central government department
EASSW	European Association of Schools of Social Work
ERASMUS	A European Union-funded programme to promote mobility for education staff and students – now superseded by SOCRATES
FBT	(Germany) Fachbereichstag Soziale Arbeit (Germany) – an organization of some 70 member institutions that offer degrees in social work (previously known under the initials KFS)
GDP	Gross Domestic Product
GDR	German Democratic Republic
HBO	(Netherlands) Hoger Beroepsonderwijs – a prescribed level of higher professional education
HBO-Raad	(Netherlands) Association of Dutch Polytechnics and Colleges
HSAO	(Netherlands) Hoger Sociaal Agogisch Onderwijs – Higher Education in Social and Community Work
IASSW	International Association of Schools of Social Work
ICSW	International Council for Social Welfare

IEFP	(Portugal) Institute of Employment and Professional Training ·
IPSS	(Portugal) Instituições Particulares de Solidariedade Social – social services institutions part-funded by the state
ISSS	(Portugal) Institute of Social Work Education
MWD	(Netherlands) Social Work and Community Services
NAP	(Portugal) Pedagogic Support Team
NAPO	(UK) National Association of Probation Officers
OECD	Organisation for Economic Co-operation and Development
PenA	(Netherlands) Personnel and Labour Relations
PEPT	(Portugal) Education for All Programme
PIPSE	(Portugal) Interministerial Programme for the Promotion of Educational Success
PQSW	(UK) Post-Qualifying Award in Social Work
PSR	(UK) Pre-Sentence Report – a report prepared for a court on an offender prior to sentence
RIAGG	(Netherlands) Regional Institute for Outpatient Mental Health Care
SDF	(Denmark) Social Development Funds
SJD	(Netherlands) Social Rights Services
SOCRATES	A European Union-funded programme to promote mobility for education staff and students – previously, a similar programme was known as ERASMUS
SPH	(Netherlands) Social and Pedagogical Work
SPO	(Portugal) Psychology and Guidance Service
SSD	(UK) Social Services Department
TACIS	A European Union-funded programme to promote the development of countries in Eastern Europe
TEMPUS	A European Union-funded programme to promote the development of countries in Eastern Europe
USL	(Italy) Unitià Sanitarie Locali – local health administrative units

Name index

Subject index

185